PAVLOV'S IDIOTS

PAVLOV'S IDIOTS

TURNING DAY TO DAY CYCLES INTO REALIZED DREAMS

MRS. SUSAN AMATO

CONTENTS

CHAPTER ONE-THE CYCLE OF NEGATIVE

THEMES

CHAPTER EIGHT-RECONDITIONING MY TRUE AUTHENTIC SELF

CHAPTER NINE-RECONDITIONING THE POWER OF FAITH

CHAPTER TEN-RECONDITIONING WHO AM I?

CHAPTER ELEVEN-DREAM ON AND NEVER GIVE UP

CHAPTER TWELVE-DREAMS REALLY DO COME TRUE!

DEDICATION

This book is dedicated to two of the greatest men I have ever known. The first being my deceased father, Dr. Robert Edwin Drennan, Jr., who was a fantastic mental health counselor, who I wanted to be just like, and the second one being my precious husband, the love of my life, Dr. Richard Stanley Amato. I call him *"Doc"*. Doc is my best friend, an expert on the brain disease of addiction, and a person I have admired my entire life.

These two men have been the most influential people in my life who taught me, through life experience, much of what was needed to write this book. The three of us together give all of the credit to God, who reveals all things. In addition, I dedicate this book to my three children: Michael, Megan and Andrew whom I love with all my heart and hope will grow up knowing they have indescribable worth! Lastly, I dedicate this book to my mom, Eloise Drennan who has supported me in everything I've ever done. And, I dedicate this to her for being the best

mother hen to both her children and grandchildren.

INTRODUCTION

Many may wonder why a title of such nature was chosen. Most of us at some point in our lives can say we have felt like an *idiot*. Don't be offended by the title of this book. The word **idiot** means **mentally handicapped.**[1]

This book will reveal that much like Pavlov using dogs as machines, we were raised to be like machines. We have all received impairments, blockages and restrictions to our dreams coming true. *It can feel as if there has been a force against us since birth.* Our experiences in life, conditioned by human beings left us handicapped, yet the power of the human organs of the heart and brain have allowed us to change these handicaps to be effective, happy, free individuals who experience peace as they find that dreams really do come true!

This book is for those who are lost, stuck, and simply feel hopeless and unsatisfied living in the day to day cycle called life. Don't lose hope! This book will show you how you can overcome the way you were conditioned in childhood and be reconditioned to meet a new you, one who is experiencing a new reality, *living the life of your dreams.*

Somewhere between 1890 and 1930 Russian physiologist **Ivan Pavlov** discovered a phenomenon known as ***"classical conditioning"*** which would change the way we see human behavior for the rest of time. Pavlov studied the behavior of dogs and we now know that much like the conditioning of dogs, humans are conditioned too!

Pavlov rang a bell before he would feed the dogs. He soon noticed when he rang the bell, the dogs had a reflex response of salivating upon the presentation of food. Pavlov labeled the dog's response ***"psychic reflex"*** and won a Nobel Prize for this amazing discovery.

With human behavior, we may consider the reflex of the dogs similar to when something happens around us and it elicits a response in us as if something else is going to happen. Pavlov discovered that people associate two stimuli and they react to the one stimulus as if it were the other stimuli.

It would be like a man having an abusive mother who compliments him one minute, then tears him down the next. Later in life, when he marries a very nice young lady, instead of accepting his wife's compliments, he cringes after she compliments him. He then expects her to be like his mother and tear him down afterwards. To protect himself, he keeps a wall up between them. His wife can never get close to him and he is afraid to get close to his wife. The conditioning of his childhood experience left him with an unnecessary *handicap* in marriage.

It is a fact that all humans have been conditioned and this has had both a positive and negative impact on all of our lives. Most of us don't see things for what they really are. Instead we have a perception of how we think things are. Much like a dog can learn to associate food to the ringing of a bell, we as human beings are conditioned from a time before we can even remember to perceive life a certain way. This is what left us with a *handicap*.

Just like Pavlov may have used dogs as machines for his experiments, our backgrounds have shaped us to become much like a robot or a machine. In the psychology world we call it a ***script***. The messages we received as children, through our experiences, created a script for us which we seem to fulfill and continuously repeat. We are not merely conditioned to salivate when we see food but are conditioned by many negative experiences from flawed humans who gave us negative messages. While human experiences with parents may feel like fact, it is still human experience flawed by imperfection.

This book will transform your life forever! The goal of this book is to identify how we were conditioned so that we can recondition ourselves to be productive members of society who see our dreams come true. Through the counseling stories in this book, **that have been altered for people's privacy**, you will receive the tools needed to experience the joy, peace and happiness you deserve. My hope is that you may become free to dream and believe in what you want as you become who you really are, the real authentic you instead of the *conditioned* you. The concepts in this book changed my life. It consists of a lifetime of counseling experience.

Chapter 1-The Cycle of Negative Themes

CONDITIONING IS REAL

Between the average age of eighteen months and three years old we learn a language. Most of us do not remember learning our native language perhaps, which could be English. We do not remember our dad or mom saying, *"Say da-da or say ma-ma,"* yet by the time we have reached three or four years old, we speak English fluently. ***We became fluent in our native language and we cannot remember learning it.*** The same is said to be true that we became fluent in a negative language we do not remember learning. This negative language, just like English, became so engrained in us that we don't remember learning it, we don't know we speak it, and we don't know we perceive negative messages about ourselves because of it. This is called our

negative theme. We became mentally handicapped at such an early age. We have been conditioned to receive negative messages from childhood, even if the people around us had no intention of giving us these messages. The negative messages received became our negative theme. ***We are all mentally handicapped by having a negative theme. We do not know we have a negative theme and we don't remember learning it.***

If you were to be put in a gym with people speaking one hundred languages, no matter what was said, you would only understand your native language. With your negative theme, it would be like, no matter what is being said, all you hear is, *"I am inadequate,"* or *"I am worthless,"* or *"They don't love me."* Rest assured, in this chapter, you will uncover your personal *handicap* and you will learn how to manage it so that you can experience the freedom, joy and inner peace you deserve, within yourself and in your relationship with others.

7

THE HANDICAP OF NEGATIVE

THEMES

❖ A little lady found herself a suicidal adult because she heard most of her life by her mom-"*I wish you were not born. I wish I would have gotten an abortion.*" This produced in her a **worthless theme.**

❖ A man found himself very depressed as an adult. When looking back, he saw that both of his parents had been workaholics. When he left for school, no one was home. When he came home from school, no one was home at night. This produced in him an **unimportant theme.**

❖ A lady found herself feeling very anxious as an adult. She came to understand that both of her parents had criticized her most of her life. This produced in her an ***inadequate theme.*** Although these experiences happened in childhood, they carried over into adulthood negative messages that affected their daily lives. Messages received from parents and our experiences feel like fact, yet scientific fact shows how others treat us is about them not us.

All three of these people came to realize that there was a negative theme from childhood driving their negative feelings as an adult. They took the time to recondition how they viewed themselves and started experiencing a positive new life. Before we can change our handicap, we need to know what the handicap is. What is your negative theme?

7 QUESTIONS-IDENTIFY YOUR

NEGATIVE THEME

1. What was your primary negative feeling as a child?

2. What is your primary negative feeling now as an adult?

3. What was the negative belief you had of yourself as a child?

4. What is the negative belief you have of yourself now as an adult?

5. What negative message did you receive about yourself from your father as a child?

6. What negative message did you receive about yourself from your mother as a child?

7. How did the worst trauma of your childhood leave you feeling about yourself?

The answers to these questions will most likely be similar, as they are revealing your negative theme. This book was not written to shame you. This book was written to show you that you have undiscovered worth. It is my job to show you, like Pavlov discovered dogs were conditioned, we have been conditioned too. It is time to recondition you, to the new you. We all have a negative theme, perceive life through a negative lens, and believe negative messages that are lies about ourselves.

THE TRUTH ABOUT OTHERS

If your dad never had time for you, something was wrong with him. If your mother criticized you, her self-esteem was probably wrapped up so much in you that she had no self-love of her own. If your parent told you they wish you were not born, it is because they wish *they* were not born. It is impossible to be worthless, unimportant, or even inadequate. To believe these lies will put us in the position of being a machine or a robot versus a person

11

with feelings who is here on the Earth for a specific reason.

THE TRUTH ABOUT US

The truth is each one of us has a fingerprint that is one out of eight billion, a masterpiece, different from everyone else. Your DNA reflects a special identity known through your saliva, your eyes, your teeth and your fingerprints. Your worth is indescribable! The hard-core proven fact is that *there is no other human being on the Earth like you!* We cannot compare ourselves to any other individual as it is impossible. We are not them and they are not us, yet somehow we all connect.

THE TRUTH ABOUT INVENTORS

Inventors are passionate dreamers who work often from scratch tirelessly to complete an expected result. They want to achieve a completely unique purpose, to manifest a radical breakthrough that will change history and make an astronomical difference in the lives of others. It is obvious that when a person invents something, he has a purpose in mind. Long ago, people sat on floors, so a man invented a chair. Imagine how excited he must have been to make life so much more comfortable. When he invented a chair, he likely said, *"Here is how the chair works, sit in it like this."* What purpose would it serve for us to turn the chair upside down and sit on the legs? The purpose of the chair would not be achieved, to have a comfortable place to sit. Who are we to tell the inventor how we should sit in the chair? Alike, whoever made you had a purpose. Who are you to tell your inventor that you have no worth? Perhaps our inventor was passionate about us, made us from scratch, and wants to manifest a radical breakthrough with us that will change history and make an astronomical difference in our lives as well.

Understanding your worth is the necessary piece to give you drive for your destiny. Not accepting your worth would be like sitting on the upside-down chair, misusing the reason you are here. Having a *handicap* certainly makes it harder to experience living life to the maximum of our potential. Just like other inventors, our inventor had a very specific plan when he made us, and excitedly waits to show us our particular purpose and expected result.

YOU HAVE WORTH! It is time to dream, believe and see your dreams come true. Going 'round and round' on a hamster's wheel, given we are supposed to live an average life span of eighty years is not an acceptable option. We can't live eighty years miserably. We need change and we need change *now*.

Which do you prefer? To live eighty years with an unnecessary impediment, seeing yourself as worthless, or knowing you have worth and are living your life to the maximum of your potential? We must reject the lies of worthlessness, inadequacy, feeling unimportant, and dare

14

to dream and believe in our worth. We must take the time to identify the negative language we are speaking and perceiving, and we must make a daily effort to change it and learn a new language. Now say it to yourself, **"I have worth."** Don't worry you will get used to it. We must begin the reconditioning process, so we can live life, on the Earth, abundant-*now*!

CHANGE OUR SELF TALK

1. Dispute the lie i.e. *"I am worthless."*
2. Replace it with the truth i.e. *"I am not worthless. I have worth."*
3. Repeat it until you believe it.

We need to begin the lifelong process of changing how we speak to ourselves. Once we start changing our *self-talk*, slowly but surely, we will start to believe the truth. If a little girl was told by her mother, *"I wish you were never born,"* and the little girl heard this all throughout her life, she would no doubt feel worthless. Yet, if we asked a crowd, *"Do you think this woman is worthless,"* we would say, *"no of course not!"* This lady would have to face the painful fact that something was wrong with her mother. She would see that she learned the emotion of worthlessness and it is a part of her daily experience. The sad part is that she was conditioned this way; however, there is hope for her to recondition her view of herself as she faces the truth about her mother. We must work daily to speak positively to ourselves.

Like this lady, many of our lives are at stake because of the negative messages we have believed. Some have turned to addictive behaviors such as drugs, alcohol, sex, or pornography, while others distract themselves through helping others, work, food or any other method to numb or comfort. Many people end up suicidal and many people simply just co-exist in marriages and stay in abusive relationships. Sometimes the very messages we believe about ourselves puts our very existence at stake. *This is why it is imperative to uncover what we have been believing about ourselves and change it.*

THREE TYPES OF RELATIONSHIPS

Those who speak English speak it to themselves, to others and to God. Those who speak another language speak it to themselves, to others and to God. We have three types of relationships. We have a relationship with our *self*, with *others* and with *God*. Whatever our negative learned language, we also *speak* and *perceive it* with our selves, others and God.

1. *I with myself* - Have you ever thought about how your relationship is going with yourself? My daughter Megan kept a poster in her room that said, *"I may as well be myself because everyone else is taken."* The most important assignment in our lives is to take care of our *self*. You can take

out a journal and reflect on these questions: Are you good to yourself? Do you talk nice to yourself? Do you listen to yourself? How do you feel about yourself? If we discovered our negative theme was worthless and we start to monitor how we speak to ourselves, we will notice that our speech will reflect negative connotation insinuating we are worthless. It is our job to identify how we are speaking to ourselves and to change it. We need to become our own best friend and begin to take care of ourselves, like we might a three-year-old precious child, who is dependent upon us.

2. *I with others* - Have you ever stopped to think about what we tell ourselves regarding others? Have you ever stopped to think when someone doesn't text back what words you say to yourself? Perhaps you say, *"They don't like me,"* (I am worthless) or *"Maybe I said something that upset*

them," (I am inadequate) or *"I knew they wouldn't text,"* (I am unimportant) or perhaps another response. The same negative message we believe of ourselves will be the words we tell ourselves others are saying about us, even if it is not true. ***We have to train ourselves not to mind read or guess what others are thinking.*** Most of the time what we are guessing is wrong. Take out your journal and reflect on the following questions: What am I telling myself that the grocery store lady/boss/employees/relatives/children/spouse thinks of me? We tell ourselves awful things regarding other people, things that are simply not true. Any time we are tempted to guess, we need to tell ourselves the truth, that we *don't know* what they are thinking and what they are thinking is none of our business. Most people aren't thinking of you. They are thinking of themselves.

3. *I with God* - After counseling many couples and discovering their negative themes, the way they answered the question, *"What do you think God thinks of you?"* was rather fascinating and disturbing. Without fail, my clients gave an answer that matched their negative theme. One man who felt unimportant his whole life said, *"I don't think God thinks of me."* He didn't think he was important to God. One woman described an angry judgmental God that seemed to criticize her, just like her mother. One man who was severally beaten as a child proceeded to tell me, *"God is not real"* and then added, *"if he was real, he would want nothing to do with me. He would think I am a worthless piece of crap."* He then proceeded to describe more thoughts about God that seemed to perfectly describe the stepfather who beat him. He in fact thought God saw him like his stepfather saw him.

The fact that people were perceiving the Higher Power much like their human experience fascinated me and also concerned me deeply. I thought, *could it be that people are robbed of a God who may love them and have a destiny for them because of their warped perception, coming from their human earthly experience, called their negative theme?* Take a moment with your journal and ask yourself, *"What does God think of me?"* Your answer may surprise you. Once we find that our answer matches our negative theme, we will be able to see **there may be a Higher Power out there, entirely different from what we imagined, who feels more about us than we realized.**

Once we identify the messages, we are saying to ourselves, we need to capture those thoughts and change them. **If we want to see something better, we must think differently and "say" something more positive to** *ourselves.* There is great power in knowing that we have worth. The way we speak towards ourselves needs to reflect our worth. Seeing yourself differently and changing your *self-talk* will prove to give you better results.

Take some time to look at yourself and evaluate your life. *Does the music you listen to promote worth or worthlessness? Do the people or groups you interact with promote your worth or show you that you are worthless? Does your relationship with your spouse promote you are worthy or promote worthlessness? Does the job you have promote your gifts and show you have worth, or does it make you feel unimportant or worthless?*

Do not be an idiot who accepts an unnecessary mental handicap. Do not receive the bad labels or the negative messages received in trauma or life's experiences. Believe what Ivan Pavlov discovered about conditioning. ***It is a fact that you have been conditioned negatively and that is what is wrong with you***. You were conditioned with a negative theme. Now believe you can be *reconditioned*. You have the power to believe you have worth.

My life has never been the same since I realized I was conditioned with a negative theme. I became floored, by the fact, I viewed life through a very specific lens. Soon thereafter, I realized I had undiscovered power to be reconditioned. The ability to see and think differently became apparent. My hope is that you will hold on, through the details of this book, to find the treasure of discovering the authentic you. While the first six chapters will reveal details on how you have been conditioned, the remaining chapters will help you discover who you really are and help you get to where you would like to go. The next chapter will reveal exactly why you think the way you do, so that you can begin to see and think something different, getting you one step closer to realizing dreams.

Chapter 2-The Cycle of Interpolation

Now that you know you have a *handicap* called a negative theme, we will look at a very important word called *interpolation*. *This is when we take data from our past experience and project it onto our present experience to make a guess about what we think is happening.* The cycle of *interpolation* is one of the greatest ways we can be an **idiot**. The **handicap** of *interpolation* is astronomically paralyzing because most of the time, we guess wrong. We must take another step and remove the cycle of interpolation from the way we live to get closer to realizing our dreams.

INTERPOLATION AND METEOROLOGY

Have you ever wondered why your local meteor-ologist says on TV that it is going to snow ten inches, yet it doesn't snow at all? ***When we interpolate, we make an educated guess where we have no facts from a place where we have facts.***[2] Let's imagine we are looking for the temperature for three cities. We have a thermometer (fact) in West Palm Beach, Florida and it says it is 70 de-grees. In Boynton Beach, Florida we have a thermometer (fact) and it says that it is 80 degrees. In Wellington, Flor-ida, a city in between, we have no thermometer (no fact) so we *interpolate*. We make an educated guess for that city with no thermometer (no facts) from the cities we have thermometers (facts) and make a guess that it is 75 degrees. Now when we guess, we may be right, or we may be wrong. Meteorologists do this every day. If they say it is going to snow and it does not, it is because they interpolated wrong. They constantly have to guess on situations where they have no facts from the other places where they received facts. Where we live in Florida, we get hurricanes. The meteorologists are constantly interpolating regarding the storms. For those on the ocean, if the meteorologist interpolates (guesses) there will be a hurricane, a person prepares with lots of food and water. They may board their windows or even evacuate. If the meteorologist was wrong and the hurricane never came, they were prepared, and nothing was lost. If the meteorologist guessed a hurricane was not coming their way and it did come, interpolating wrong could cost a person his life. Most people prepare either way and take the road of caution.

INTERPOLATION AND MATHEMATICS

When working with the intelligence community, while counseling in the state of Maryland, the engineers who worked at NASA would reference *interpolation*. I would hear things like ***"if we interpolate right, the space-ship will make it to the moon and if we interpolate wrong it will explode in the air."*** See the diagram to understand how engineers use interpolation, according to Wikipedia.

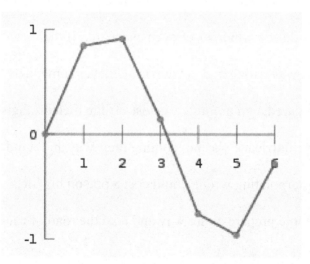

"In the mathematical field of numerical analysis, interpolation is a method of constructing new data points within the range of a discrete set of known data points."[2]

Figure 1. Plot of the data with linear interpolation super-imposed. Adapted from "Interpolation," by Berland, 2007. Retrieved February 9, 2019, from https://en.wikipedia.org/wiki/Interpolation. Copyright 2019 by Wikipedia.

Therefore, to simplify this, those from NASA sending spaceships to the moon will take places where there are facts and then make an educated guess where there are *no* facts. **If they guess correctly, the spaceship will make it to the moon, and if they guess incorrectly, it will explode in the air.** What do our engineers and meteorologists do to improve the way they interpolate? Over the years they have changed and perfected ways to assimilate data. This is exactly what we need to do. *We need to change the ways we assimilate data into our everyday lives,* considering relationships can be the same way.

INTERPOLATION AND RELATIONSHIPS

Interpolation can be the silent killer in relationships. **Our experience and the messages from our parents feel like fact.** If a little boy is beaten by his father, he assumes he is worthless. When he grows older, he will take those messages that felt like facts and he will make a guess by thinking others think he is worthless as well. We take our parents' opinion, experiences and negative messages from childhood and we carry them into today. *We spend most of our adult life believing the negative messages that people told us about ourselves when we were little.* We do this our whole entire lives and those around us are doing it. We have been conditioned with messages, just like dogs salivate when they hear a bell ring when they are expecting food. We received a negative message as a child, so we perceive that message. Just like meteorologists and engineers who guess based on their facts, we can be wrong, also.

We interpolate before we can even remember. Let us look at a systematic process of how interpolation takes place. A five-year-old little girl was attending Kindergarten. Halfway through the school year, when her teacher asked her to read, she was able to stumble through to the end of a paragraph. When the little girl finished reading, before the teacher was able to say anything, the little girl thought to herself, *"I don't think I read very well."* She thought this because she was raised by a mom who corrected and criticized her all the time. This made her feel inadequate. Her mom's opinion of her felt like fact, therefore, when she read, she figured her teacher would think she didn't read well. Did the teacher think she did a bad job? Was the little girl's guess right or wrong? All of a sudden, the teacher spoke up and said, *"You did a fantastic job reading!"* The little girl was very surprised. The teacher was so proud because six months prior to this she didn't know how to read at all. The little girl was wrong about her interpolation based on her past experience and often, we are too. **When we guess wrong, we put ourselves through an unnecessary, emotional rollercoaster.**

LEARNING ABOUT INTERPOLATION

My father, Robert Edwin Drennan, Jr., truly is one of my two heroes in life. He was a counselor and I studied under him since I was very young. He left a fantastic legacy and was a great model for me to follow. Since age thirteen, he took me to many counseling groups, and it was then I made up my mind I wanted to be like him by going into the same occupation as him. There were over 500 people at his funeral, and I had the privilege of sitting there for hours while many people went up and testified how he had helped them. And he was my dad! He was the one who taught me about interpolation and showed me through stories how it occurred within the interactions of human beings. My dad taught me that *all behavior makes sense,* and while it is no excuse, people do things and believe the things they believe for a reason. The people attending my father's funeral were asked to leave the church that night when it went hours over because of the continuous testimonies. The church had another event coming in. He was one of the smartest people I have ever known. I am so thankful to have had the privilege to study under *the wisdom of a grey-haired man.*

EXPERIENCE AND INTERPOLATION

This is a classic story of interpolation. Some details have been altered. Believe it or not this happens a lot. A husband and wife came in for counseling. The husband was very confused. The counselor asked what brought them in. The husband replied, *"Last night I gave my wife a dozen red roses and the night was horrible."* The husband explained that his wife was very angry at him, cursing at him, throwing things and kept saying, *"I can't believe you did that!"* The husband said, *"Did what?"* The wife just wailed and couldn't seem to get out what she felt her husband did. They ended up in the counseling session the next day. This was a classic case of interpolation. When this happens, both persons involved need to give each other the benefit of the doubt. The counselor found out that when the wife was a little girl, her dad brought her mom a dozen red roses every time he had cheated on her. So, the wife *interpolated* when she took the facts of her past experience and projected them onto her current situation. She guessed her husband cheated, however, she guessed wrong. This may sound like your story.

The counselor worked with both of them to heal the past, so they could have a healthy relationship in their marriage. Can you imagine the feelings that woman experienced for no reason? Her husband loved her very much. He was patient with her past and worked with his wife and the counselor to heal that trauma. When we interpolate wrong, it not only affects ourselves, but it affects those we are interacting with. ***Make a decision, starting now, that you will do your best not to allow yourself to experience emotions based on your guess before you find out the real facts.*** Break out of the cycle of interpolation when you feel something negative by identi-

fying your feelings and checking it out by the following

steps before you react.

TOOLS FOR INTERPOLATION
I AM-WHO I AM

1. Identify how you feel and accept the truth of

    how you feel. When you get in touch with

    your feelings then you can deal with them. The

    rose lady may have to say, *"Receiving a dozen*

    roses is a trigger and I feel scared."

2. Ask about your assumptions. Never assume!

    Instead of guessing, ***check it out***. Your trauma

    and life's experiences are a part of you. There

    is no reason to be ashamed of how you feel or

    what you have been through. Let those who

    love you know what you are going through.

The rose lady may have to say, *"Are you cheating?"*

3. **M**irror to yourself and others the truth. The rose lady may have to look herself in the mirror a million times and tell herself the truth, *"My husband actually loves me, and he is not cheating."*

Accepting ourselves is extremely important even if our thinking may seem insane. Identifying how we feel gets us closer to knowing ourselves. As we begin to see that we have been plagued by a negative theme and we have lived daily seeing circumstances through that lens, it can be a relief when we begin to see how much of it, we can change. To do otherwise robs us of our dreams. Guessing wrong was a hinderance and now *checking it out* will be an advantage. We begin to see we really are important, and our lives are really going to change.

For me, understanding interpolation allowed me to get to know myself and others better. It has been extremely helpful for me to know, that no matter what people say, we perceive what they say in a certain way. Sometimes I hear right and other times I hear wrong. People are not always saying what we think they are saying. Knowing we all make a guess about our current situations, based on our previous experiences, has caused me to do a lot more listening. It became my job to understand both myself as well as others.

In the next chapter, we will look at the subjects of anger, anxiety and depression. These are the three symptoms people live with that debilitate their daily lives. The great news is that there is an undiscovered power that will be revealed regarding these symptoms, unleashing those blocks to realizing dreams.

Chapter 3-The Cycle of Negative Belief

ANGER, ANXIETY AND DEPRESSION

The three greatest symptoms of negative beliefs come through anger, anxiety and depression. *Anger* is an outward expression of a belief I cannot handle. *Anxiety* is a nervous expression of a belief I cannot handle. *Depression* is an inward expression of a belief I cannot handle. These symptoms seem to debilitate people's lives, exhausting and weakening them to the point of not being able to produce. If you are experiencing any of these, you are experiencing a belief that you cannot handle. Your body is telling you that something is wrong.

Anger, anxiety, and depression can definitely be a *handicap*. This can leave us hopeless when, in fact, there is much hope. Discovering what is wrong and fixing it can be simple. Experiencing these symptoms and not dealing with what is wrong can make us ***idiots,*** leaving us with a ***handicap***. This chapter will give you the answers that you need in order to deal with anger, anxiety, and depression moving you closer to realized dreams.

TWO TYPES OF BELIEFS

There are only two types of beliefs; core belief and situational belief. A ***core belief*** might be something you have believed for a long, long time. It may be your negative theme learned in childhood. A child who is criticized his entire life by a parent could believe he can never do anything right. This would be an example of a core belief of inadequacy. Having the core belief *"I am inadequate"* may give a person a handicap in life. ***Our core*** *belief can be identified by the seven questions on negative themes in chapter one.*

A *situational belief* would be something we end up believing because of a situation that has happened. There was once a woman whose son-in-law left her daughter. This woman was a good woman, but she was so angry at how her daughter was treated that she wanted to kill her son-in-law. This woman's rage had to do with herself. A situation happened, she felt angry, but she had no knowledge that her anger came from a belief she had of herself. The belief could be true, or it could be a lie.

Just because we believe something, doesn't make it true. I led her through the steps written below to identify her belief. The first step we need to take to deal with our beliefs coming from anger, anxiety, and depression is to identify what the belief is. This can be the hardest step. Once you identify how you feel, you can proceed with the following steps to identify the belief. The steps in the following exercise can be followed for any situation.

STEP ONE - IDENTIFY THE BELIEF I CANNOT HANDLE

With an example from the story above

How do you feel? *"I feel angry."*

Identify the belief you cannot handle by asking yourself the following question:

What does that mean? (your anger) *"My son-in law left my daughter."*

What does that mean? (the son-in-law left your daughter) *"My grandchildren are hurt."*

What does that mean? (your grandchildren are hurt) *"I couldn't protect them."*

What does that mean? (you couldn't protect them) *"I am inadequate."*

*when you come to an I statement + a feeling word you are at the belief *

Next ask yourself the following question: IS THIS TRUE OR A LIE?

Once the lady got in touch with her belief, she never had thoughts of murder again. She disputed the lie that she was inadequate. The entire family dealt with the trauma of the situation. The children healed and later the mother married a man who was the greatest husband and stepparent to her children. Eventually, they saw that the pain of this situation turned into an unexpected blessing.

STEP TWO - IS THE BELIEF TRUE OR A LIE?

The belief was *"I am inadequate."* Next, ask yourself if this is the truth or a lie. This is a lie. A person must dispute the lie in order to feel better. *A person will know she has identified the belief she cannot handle when her statement comes to an "I" statement with a feeling word.* We have the power to do something about our symptoms of anger, anxiety, and depression. When the person was able to get rid of the lie *"I am inadequate"* because she could not protect her daughter or grandchildren, then she became rational, was thinking clearly, and was then able to truly be there to help her daughter.

STEP THREE - MAKE A CHANGE

The first step is to *identify the belief.* Once the belief is identified, then we take the second step and figure out *if the belief is true or a lie* and then we can take the third step and *do something with the belief.* If the belief is a *lie,* we must make a *COGNITIVE* (thinking) change to get a feeling change. *Most of the time the negative beliefs we believe are lies.* If the belief is *true,* we must make a *BEHAVIORAL* change to get a feeling change. Sometimes we will find what we are angry, anxious or depressed about is the truth. Making this behavioral or cognitive change will cause our symptoms of anger, anxiety, or depression to dissipate.

THE BELIEF IS A LIE

There was a woman who felt like she was having panic attacks, which is anxiety. She was a young woman in her twenties. She went through these steps to figure out why she was anxious. After years of hard work, she had finally become debt free with her credit cards, however, the day came when her car broke down, and she had to put $2,500 on a credit card. When she sat with her anxiety, instead of avoiding it, she realized she believed two things. First, she believed she was going to be homeless. I said, *"What! How?"* She got in touch that her belief was because of her new credit card debt. I asked her if she was able to make the minimum payment monthly on the credit card and she said, *"Yes."* Therefore, she was believing a lie. As soon as she got in touch with the fact, she wouldn't be homeless, her panic and anxiety went away. She went through the following steps:

1. Dispute the lie. *"I am not going to be homeless."*
2. Replace it with the truth. *"I can afford the minimum payment."*
3. Repeat it until I believe it.

This may sound ridiculous; however, we all experience irrational thinking much more than we would like to admit. The second belief she was having was that she was inadequate. I asked her to help me understand that. She stated it was because she was already back in credit card debt again. We talked about simple options of saving money and certain lifestyles to help her stay debt free. She came to realize she was believing the lie of inadequacy because, in fact, she had been doing the best she could. This brought us to see that inadequacy was a common theme of hers due to childhood where she felt she was expected to be perfect most of her life. This inadequate feeling was no doubt one of her core beliefs.

Gabriella, my daughter's friend says, ***"There are no limits on what you can accomplish, except the limits you*** *put on your own thinking."* We had found her root issue. She then learned while we were working on her root issue that she would have to continue to dispute those lies daily and replace them with the truth daily until her core language changed to feeling adequate. Once again, she practiced the aforementioned steps.

THE BELIEF IS TRUE

A young man woke up one to day to realize he was feeling very depressed, so he decided he would go to therapy for his depression. He went to therapy and the therapist asked him why he was depressed. He looked down at himself and said, *"I have kept myself very busy most of my life. I have been less busy recently, woke up one day, looked at myself and realized I am depressed because **I am overweight**."* Given he was 495 pounds, the **truth** was that he was medically obese. He would not be able to dispute the lie and replace it with the truth because it was true. In this case, **when we believe something negative**

and it is true, we must make a behavioral change to feel

better. We must make a behavioral change to lessen the

symptoms of anger, anxiety or, in his case, depression.

1. Accept the truth. "*I am overweight.*"
2. Come up with a behavioral change to produce a feeling change. (nutritionist, exercise)
3. Continue behavioral changes until desired outcome manifests.

Interestingly enough, within a few weeks he told the

therapist, *"I don't want to lose weight."* The therapist

was surprised but knew he must have a good reason. He

confessed he had been sexually abused as a child and his

perpetrator had always told him what a handsome boy he

was when he was younger. He got in touch with the fact,

he used food as a means to cover himself up, so he would

no longer be handsome, as he felt being handsome was

the cause of his abuse. Being overweight and feeling safe

outweighed the fact he didn't feel good about himself.

After he confessed this abuse, he told me he had felt worthless ever since he was abused.

COGNITIVE AND BEHAVIORAL CHANGES

Two beliefs were uncovered from this situation. *"I am overweight,"* which was a true statement, and the second one was, *"I am worthless"* because of the abuse. **This belief was a lie.** Yes, he was fat, but he was not worthless. Since he was uninterested in losing weight at that point, he and the therapist dealt with his core belief of worthlessness. Through a very lengthy process, the man used the aforementioned exercise daily to help him manage his symptoms of depression while he and the therapist did a lot of regression and recovery work regarding the abuse. He made daily thinking changes for years until having thoughts of worth became his lifestyle.

The day came where the overweight man came into the session and told the therapist he was ready to lose weight. Therefore, we know he will need to make a be-havioral change. He soon then found a nutritionist, started exercising, and eating healthier. He realized the more work he did to heal from the abuse, the more he became motivated to get healthier. Within a year he had lost two hundred pounds and continued to lose weight after that more slowly. Every day he made behavioral changes to get him to his desired outcome. Every day he made think-ing changes as he disputed the lies of being worthless.

Before he knew it, he had lost a lot of weight, started gaining much improved self-esteem, and this be-came a trickle-down effect in many areas of his life. He went into a new career helping teenaged boys who were troubled and abused just like he had been. His career change brought him more satisfaction than ever, and it even brought him more money! After dealing with his de-pression his pain turned into purpose.

WE HAVE THE POWER

For many years, I had more clients than I could count who came in suffering with depression. Many of these people had been depressed for fifteen to twenty years. Most of the depression was due to a core belief such as, *"I am unimportant,"* that they had felt most of their lives. These people were stuck on depression medicine and felt extremely hopeless. Once they got in touch with the negative beliefs, they had experienced their entire lives and started to believe they had worth, their symptoms of depression left them.

My niece, Christina Drennan says, **"What you were taught in the past was a lie. You must retrain yourself to see and believe the truth."** A person in my practice was in and out of the psychiatric ward, three to four times a year, with suicidal ideation before he came in. That person ended up changing his belief from being unimportant to important and his whole life changed for the better.

What we believe can make the difference between leth-

argy and energy, happy and sad, and even life or death.

We cannot afford to believe lies. *We must believe the*

truth. Each of us is a masterpiece with a purpose different

from each other.

We do not have power over many people, situa-

tions, or things; however, we do have power over anger,

anxiety, and depression. We all have negative core beliefs

that plague us from our childhood. We all have irrational

beliefs in the situations we experience. Ninety-three per-

cent of our beliefs are lies, and this can be a hinderance to

our health, happiness, peace, and productivity. We must

dispute these lies.

We don't have to be an *idiot*, deceiving ourselves

with lies, leaving us with a *handicap* making little pro-

gress or making success difficult. We can take our symp-

toms of anger, anxiety, and depression and figure out

what we believe and do something about it that will

change our lives forever. *We have the power to decide on a behavioral change or a thinking change, which will give us a feeling change.* Experiencing these symptoms will rob you from fulfilling dreams. You must seek the meaning behind them. If you come to the place where you feel you need help with anger, anxiety or depression, seek professional help to guide you along the path to realized dreams.

Now that we are learning a lot more about ourselves, it is time to reveal some interesting thoughts regarding others. When we begin to see why others do what they do it can become an asset to the way we view our circumstances. Knowing the truth about ourselves and others can free us in ways we could not have imagined. The next chapter will unveil the mystery behind why people react. In all my years of counseling, understanding reaction has been a necessary piece that has helped people get one step closer to living their dreams.

Chapter 4-The Cycle of Reaction

Reaction means *"from"* not *"to."* When someone is reacting, it's about the person reacting. Reactions can make an *idiot* of us all! Reactions look like they are towards other people but, in fact, a person reacts because the person is defending a feeling about himself due to a belief he cannot handle. To understand what reactions are and to take responsibility for our reactions will change so many aspects of our lives, freeing us from this very severe *handicap.*

EXAMPLE 1

Raised in a counselor's home, I was able to hear of many amazing stories of people my father helped.

There was a couple who came to see a therapist and there was a lot of confusion. This couple was newly married and every time the woman went to work, the husband was very upset with her. Nothing happened, and nothing was different with her work than before they were married. The husband loved his new wife and felt grateful for her yet berated her about going to work. When this happened, the wife felt *inadequate* when she went to work as if she was doing something wrong. The husband worked from home and found himself unable to concentrate on his work. This only lasted a short amount of time until the couple went to therapy.

They discovered that there was unresolved trauma for the husband. When he was a little boy, he was left alone most of the time from elementary through his high school years. Neither parent was ever home, and he remembered the sadness of his mom *leaving for work*. Now, his wife leaving for work became a ***perceived threat*** of abandonment. When the husband identified this, it was a surprise to him. He then realized that when his wife went to work, he feared she would leave him permanently. He healed from this trauma and changed his perception of his wife working. His wife was very compassionate as she realized when he was reacting, it was about him. In due time, she was able to go to work in peace.

EXAMPLE 2

A teenager with a serious drug problem felt that her mother hated her. The therapist asked why, and she said her mom would scream often and say, *"You're nothing but a drug addict," "You're a loser,"* and would call her other names. Her mother always told her she loved her, but she never believed her, instead she felt unloved.

The girl became sober and made a full recovery. After she got clean and was involved in a recovery program, she was left with unresolved feelings of the names her mom would call her when she was enraged. The therapist encouraged her to talk to her mom about it because she knew her mother's reactions were about *her mother*.

When a parent reacts to any child, they are believing something negative about their own self that they cannot handle. The girl confronted her mother, and her mother confessed that her rage was due to feeling like she was a bad mother. When the daughter understood what her mother's reaction meant, she was able to forgive her mother and dispute the negative messages she had received from the experience of her mother's rage.

EXAMPLE 3

There was a young man plagued by anxiety. His father was a perfectionist, who wanted him to wear his hair a certain way, dress a certain way, believe a certain way and act a certain way. The young man explained that he never felt he could be his own person. Interacting with his father and trying to please him became impossible. The handicap of trying to be perfect only brought him shame. *The handicap of perfectionism puts limitations on our lives and what we are able to do.*

A script like this from childhood can cause a person to be an extension of that parent and later attract and be an extension of a future spouse. This man was living as an extension of his father instead of being himself. This young man had a severe *inadequate* theme that was driving his anxiety. He ended up going to therapy and worked on his anxiety. The counselor encouraged him to find out from his father why he wanted him to be perfect.

One day, the young man got the courage to ask him. *"Dad, why did you try to make me look and act so perfect my whole life?"* The young man was astonished to hear his dad's answer. His dad was one of many children whose parents were religious addicts who lived in town. He said, *"Son, if my children are not perfect, I will receive criticism from your grandparents that will be more than I can bear, so, I try to make you or anyone else I'm involved with presentable."* The man could not believe his answer.

The man could not believe his whole life he felt inadequate thinking something was wrong with him. Even this one surprised me. When someone is reacting, it is about him or her. The anxiety and negative messages this young man had, dissipated even more quickly, when he realized the truth about his father.

EXAMPLE 4

Once I was working for a very successful business. Normally, I get along with most people. One day my boss came in screaming, "Susan, *I'm tired of all these middle school games."* Honestly, I was shocked and confused and had no idea why my boss would say such a thing. I'm typically a polite and respectful person, however, I couldn't think of anything that would illicit that type of reaction.

Instantly, I could feel that my Irish blood was boiling. Being on the verge of reacting myself, something stopped me. The thought hit-*when someone is reacting, it's about that person*. I learned my entire career that we have to have boundaries and teach people how to treat us. I proceeded to say, *"I can't do labels; however, if you would like to tell me how you feel, then I will listen."*

All of a sudden, my boss said, *"Do you remember what you said in the staff meeting this morning?"* Then he quoted *me*. He thought what I said in the staff meeting was about him. In fact, I was speaking of my deceased father. What I said was meant to be a compliment about my deceased father. My boss heard me wrong and thought I was speaking about him, which would have been an insult speaking to a person who was living as if I called him dead. His reaction was a defense for his hurt.

I apologized because I had hurt him and reassured him it was not about him and everything was fine. If I had reacted, I would have entered a cycle that could have ruined a business relationship. We need to think before we react to others reacting.

WHAT TO DO WHEN SOMEONE REACTS

I can't do _____; (reaction)
however, I can do _____.
      (what I want to see)
Communicate **"I"** not "You"

Examples of **healthy responses** to others' reactions:

❖ *I can't do yelling; however, I can talk if we can speak in a lower voice.*

❖ *I can't do silent treatments; however, when you are ready to talk, I'm ready to listen.*

❖ *I can't do blame; however, I would love to hear how you are feeling.*

❖ *I can't do abusive words; however, if you would like to tell me how you feel, I will listen.*

❖ *I can't do name calling; however, I'd like to know how you are feeling.*

Examples of **unhealthy reactions** to people's reactions:

❖ *You always yell at me. Stop yelling at me.*

❖ *You always ignore me. Talk to me right now.*

❖ *You blame me for everything but look at what you've done.*

❖ *You are the most abusive person I know. You are a low life.*

❖ *You say I'm like my mother, well you are the devil.*

When we start a sentence off with the word "you," it is considered blame. If people are reacting to us, then it is our job to not enter that cycle with them. If we then address them with a "you" statement, we end up in a cycle with them.

EXAMPLE 5

There was a depressed woman who came in to see another therapist. Her husband was very concerned about her and brought her to therapy. The therapist asked her how long she had been depressed. She said she had been depressed as long as she could remember, since she was a little girl.

The therapist asked what the husband did when his wife was depressed. He said, *"I take her to the ocean to see the boats, take her to nice dinners, buy her jewelry, buy her flowers, and try to do anything and everything to make her happy."*

The therapist asked, *"What happens when you do these nice things for her?"* The husband told of how she would get out of her depression temporarily, but then the next day she would be depressed again. The husband noticed when she got out of her depression, he felt important, but it was getting tiring as he had to constantly do something for her, and she was never happy for very long. The husband wished his wife would wonder how *he* felt sometimes and pay *him* attention.

The therapist encouraged the husband to pay his wife *no* attention when she got depressed and when she acted happy to do those nice things for her. In this case, the husband constantly rewarded his wife for her depression and subconsciously, that is why she was depressed. Neither one of them were aware of this.

When looking at her background, the woman's mom was always depressed when she was little, and her dad would rescue the mom and try to pull her out of it. Her parents modeled this cycle long before she had recollection that she learned it. This was a cycle just like Pavlov ringing a bell and feeding dogs and then noticing they would salivate. This woman would get depressed like her mom, and watch her mom get love from her dad, through her depression. This depression cycle was certainly a *handicap* and limited them from progress. Once she realized the cycle she was stuck in, she was able to get out of it and feel happy.

EXAMPLE 6

Our final example is when a little boy came in with his parents to see his male therapist. This little boy every hour, every day, no matter where he was, would crow like a rooster. It seemed as though he couldn't stop. He would stare into space and was very distant. The parents had taken this little boy to see his primary care physician, psychiatrist, and different doctors until the last resort was to see a counselor.

It was only but a couple sessions until the therapist sent the child out and kept the parents in counseling. The therapist wanted to know what was happening in the home right before the child began crowing like a rooster. The parents confessed there had been a lot of arguing between them and they were talking a lot about divorce. The therapist then realized that this eight-year-old little boy was brilliant. Ever since he started crowing like a rooster, the parents stopped talking about divorce and started concentrating on him and trying to figure out what was wrong with him.

Then the therapist bribed the little kid and said if he *didn't* crow like a rooster for one week, he would give him one hundred dollars. The little boy proved the therapist's theory; he went one week without crowing like a rooster and was given a hundred dollars. The therapist spent time with the couple and helped them get out of their negative cycle and their marriage was saved. As soon as they found out what the real problem was and dealt with it, all three of them changed. They continued on to have a very nice family.

REACTION HANDICAPS

1. Parent reaction: When reflecting upon our childhoods, we can remember many reactions of our parents that looked like they were towards us. Some of us have even been severely abused. The reactions of your parents at all times were a reflection of how they felt about themselves. *Receiving negative messages from our parent's reactions will handicap us, limiting our daily progress.*

2. Child reaction: Our children will react towards us. Even if we are trying to be the best parent we can be, when our child reacts it is a direct reflection of how the child is feeling about himself. *Giving in to children by being easily guilted will handicap us, limiting our authority as a parent.*

3. Spouse reaction: When our spouse reacts, whether it be in a passive or aggressive way, it is a direct reflection of how our spouse is feeling about him or herself. *Blaming ourselves for our spouse's reactions will handicap us, keeping us from our own personal growth.*

4. Coworker/other reaction: It doesn't matter who we are dealing with- a boss, a coworker, employees, neighbors, relatives, friends. If they are reacting even speaking abusively towards us, it is a direct parallel of how they are feeling about themselves. *Taking responsibility for other's reactions will handicap us, adding stress to our daily lives.*

5. God reaction: When bad things happen, and we think God took something or even took someone we loved from us, we may think it is because we are *bad,* and we deserved it. Perhaps we may think God hates us. When we believe God has reacted, it

is a direct reflection of Himself. He may do things we don't understand for a Higher purpose we may never know the reason for. ***Blaming God can be a devastating handicap, paralyzing us from moving forward and making progress.***

6. I with myself reaction: We get in our own way when we react. Whether we are abusive towards others or silent and hold things in, we all react. ***Blaming others for our reactions, instead of taking responsibility, will keep us stuck and rob us of our dreams coming true.***

What makes the biggest ***idiot*** with the greatest ***handicap*** is when another person is reacting, and we think it is about ourselves. When another person reacts, he or she is defending a negative feeling about him or herself. The next time someone reacts, place the imaginary author of this book on your shoulder and hear her say, ***"This is about that person."*** When we think it is about us, we are nowhere close to the truth. **Dr. Phil McGraw says,** *"My dad used to say, 'You wouldn't worry so much about what people thought of you, if you knew how seldom they did.'"* [3] When we are not seeing the truth, we are handicapped and limited as to how we can make things better. When *you* react to any person or even God, remind yourself, *"This is about me"*.

Take out your journal and write down some of the ways you have reacted and figure out what feeling you were defending about yourself.

Accepting the truth behind reactions will bring us a lot closer to realizing dreams. When we react, we feel something. Once we uncover the feelings behind our reaction, we can do something constructive about it. When others react, we no longer need to waste time by accepting responsibility for something that is not ours. Understanding reaction is half the battle involved in having a successful relationship.

Understanding reaction has been the most helpful concept learned, throughout my practice. For me personally, to understand when people are reacting it is about them has been a relief. Knowing this is the case has taken much pressure off of me. Most of my life, I was plagued by feeling responsible for how others felt. Giving up responsibility for others, as well as, understanding that people react by defending themselves took a huge weight off my back. I no longer believed negative messages about myself when others would react.

The next chapter will bring to light, how two people, with two different backgrounds and experiences can become successful in any relationship, especially the relationship of marriage. Hang on tight as the light is getting brighter to realizing your dreams.

Chapter 5-The Cycle of Marriage
"The Carousel Ride"

WHAT MAKES MARRIAGE DIFFICULT

Understanding this content is totally necessary to have a happy marriage. While the divorce rate seems to get higher year by year, marriage can make an *idiot* of us all. Marriage will definitely show us how severely *handicapped* we can be by showing great limits in daily progress and an obvious inability to succeed.

Having a happy marriage seems to be rare. We certainly do not seem to be born with the skill set on how to have a happy marriage. *Marriage is like this-the husband speaks Hebrew; the wife speaks Chinese; they don't know the common word for banana, and they are trying to raise their children and work their finances out.*

Many people choose either not to get married at all, live in unhappy marriages coexisting or end their marriages in divorce. Two people in the relationship, speaking two different languages, with two different backgrounds and experiences can definitely be a recipe for disaster. However, *those who have taken the time to understand the marriage cycle and change it have had great success in marriage.*

We believe one of the main things hindering a couple from having a great relationship is the negative cycle that goes on between them. We call this *"The Carousel Ride."* Carousels go 'round and around', up and down and in circles. They do not have a forward motion and do not go anywhere fast. Most couples are experiencing a similar dynamic.

In marriage counseling, we put *"The Carousel Ride"* on paper so that the couple can plainly see the dynamics of their cycle. This cycle includes looking at the reactions of each individual. ***Both people will learn the reasons why they are reacting, what their defenses mean and how to replace their unhealthy reactions with healthy communication.*** We call this getting off of the carousel ride and moving forward. Understanding this addictive cycle and changing it will enrich not only the relationship of the couple but will also enrich their relationships with others. This chapter will reveal the details of this cycle and how to change it. Understanding this will change the way you view marriage which may potentially change your life forever.

MARRIAGE AND NEGATIVE THEMES

In Chapter 1, *7 questions* were listed to identify your individual negative theme. Both husbands and wives have a negative theme. This is true of 100% of the people I have counseled or met. Now let's imagine this couple, Sally and Bill to use as our example. Sally was told her entire life, from her mother who raised her, she wished she were never born. Her mother told her that she wished she would have aborted her. Sally felt unwanted and unloved her whole entire life. Sally had a *worthless theme*.

On the other hand, Bill had parents who were positive to him when they were with him, however, they rarely spent time with him. Bill's parents were workaholics. Bill was alone before he went to school, as well as, when he returned from the school bus until late at night, most of his childhood. Bill's parents loved him and gave him everything. He had fun toys and they had lots of money, but Bill lacked time and attention from his parents. Bill had an *unimportant theme*. Bill imagined his whole life that he would marry, and he and his wife would spend much time together sharing a beautiful life together. Sally's dream was to marry a man who loved her. Long before

Bill and Sally got together, Sally had a *worthless* theme and Bill had an *unimportant* theme.

Little do couples know that their individual themes from childhood bring them many problems later in marriage. When Bill and Sally began dating, Bill showered Sally with a lot of attention, telling her how beautiful and wonderful she was and gave her gifts. Sally was very attracted to Bill and she felt his actions proved he wanted her. She was obviously still insecure, but she held on to the fact he seemed to really love her and want her. Sally paid Bill a lot of attention. As a matter of fact, Sally didn't like Bill out of her sight at all. She seemed very possessive of him and always wanted to be with him. This made Bill feel important.

In time, the insecurities people mask come to the surface. Sally felt deep in her heart she was truly **unworthy.** She began to distance herself from Bill because his love made her feel very afraid and vulnerable. Without doing

74

individual work, her *worthless* theme was so fluent it was like speaking her native language of English. She knew no different. She did not believe Bill could love her and she reacted to her fear by silencing herself and withdrawing.

As she withdrew from Bill, he felt very **unimportant** and his biggest fear of all came true. Her silence was like proof to Bill, *"See I knew it. I am unimportant."* Once again, he felt alone and was left all by himself. The more Bill felt ignored, the more he pursued Sally. The more Sally was pursued, the more she distanced herself as it brought up feelings of being **unworthy**. Bill tried harder to show Sally he wanted to be closer to her, however, it had the opposite effect. He felt more and more isolated and more and more **unimportant**.

If we think that we can just go through our marriage and look at our spouse through our lens, our experience and our belief system alone, we become a bonafide **idiot.**

Bonafide means genuine and remember idiot means *han-dicap,* therefore, we become genuinely handicapped. We must *see* our spouse through *their eyes* to even remotely make it in marriage and *accept* their reactions are about *them,* not ourselves. **When we look at others through our eyes only, we develop a real, genuine handicap limited by our perspective**.

When a couple gets married, they truly desire to feel the opposite of their negative theme, however, they don't realize, subconsciously, they migrate towards each other because of their negative theme. Their childhood script gets fulfilled as naturally as one drinks water. **Until each individual person deals with his own negative theme, the relationship can become hopeless.** In due time, this couple worked on their individual themes and when they saw the truth of their individual worth, they were set free to then love themselves and love each other. Although it was a lot of work, Bill came to the place where he accepted,

76

he was important, and Sally came to the place where she accepted, she had worth.

MARRIAGE AND NEGATIVE BELIEFS

In Chapter 3, we discussed how the negative beliefs of ourselves come from our negative theme as a child, the script we learned. What we believe of ourselves is our *core belief*; the way we were conditioned. These negative beliefs manifest through symptoms of anger, anxiety, and depression.

Often in our marriages, if our spouses are angry, anxious, or depressed, we can feel responsible for our spouse's feelings, when in fact, it is a negative belief they are experiencing about themselves. Also, when we are the spouse who is angry, anxious, or depressed, we may outwardly or inwardly blame our spouse, when in that case, it would be that we are experiencing a negative belief about ourselves.

When a person gets in touch with their negative belief, this person will have a choice to either make a *behavioral change* or a *thinking change* to feel better. Making this change will generate hope. If only one spouse makes a change to take care of self, one of two things happens; the other spouse will either join the person by getting healthy or get rid of the healthy spouse and stay unhealthy.

When a person becomes unhappy enough, he will make a change. ***Who wants to be with someone who doesn't want them? A sick person-that is who!*** Often it is our own mind that is sick–***our negative core belief of self.*** When we make changes to better ourselves, everything seems to change for the better. More often our spouse will get healthy with us. Less often, when we get healthy, those we love don't want to join us and would rather stay sick. The positive of this is that our spouse was never going to change, and the truth sets us free. It is our individual responsibility to face our negative core belief system and see the truth about ourselves.

MARRIAGE AND ABUSE

Many people I met have been severely abused in their marriages. If a person feels hopeless because they are being beaten, they will need to make a ***behavioral change***. More often than not, our ***core belief*** of self keeps us stuck in marriages, where we are abused.

Abusers can read the negative core beliefs of people and they will exploit them; they use people's insecurity to their advantage. Often when a person is being *falsely accused,* they are being accused of what the accuser is doing. For example, if someone constantly accuses you of cheating and you know you haven't, it is likely the person projected that onto you. When someone keeps *shaming* you, what he or she says about you is what he or she believes of him or herself. Many of those targeted, who get abused, are the type of people who are easily guilted. Deep inside they are kindhearted, and very empathic, yet are obviously deeply insecure.

The recipients of abuse tolerate bad behavior. Many abused victims *choose* not to face abuse, due to religious beliefs, where they were taught divorce is wrong. If this is you, the best book on divorce is by the man who trained my dad in counseling called, ***"But I didn't want a divorce" by Andre Bustanoby.*** [4] Those who fall victim to abuse often feel trapped. *Feeling* trapped *does not* mean you are trapped. ***You ARE NOT trapped; you need to take RESPONSIBILITY for the truth and do what is best for yourself.*** To do otherwise would be living a lie and would hinder you from coming to your Divine Destiny to reach your maximum potential. Living this type of lie has cost some men and women an entire lifetime and robbed them of fulfilling their dreams. Do what is right and care for yourself by doing the next right thing. Stop living with this *unnecessary handicap* now. When you are dealing with abuse, you are dealing with both ***core and situational beliefs***. If you are being abused and you feel incapable of making a *behavioral change* right now, find a licensed professional who can help you.

Situational beliefs definitely affect our marriages. Perhaps a husband is constantly unhappy. He may not even abuse his spouse, but he is unhappy all the time. His wife may be prone to try to rescue him or do things to make him happy by working harder, showering him with more attention or doing nice things for him. In due time, this will wear her out and neither of them will be happy.

In cases like this, the person who is with the unhappy spouse must let him go, perhaps pray for him, and wake up every day and choose to be happy, even if their spouse is not. In due time, the unhappy spouse will most likely join the happier road or become disinterested in the happy spouse. ***It is up to each individual in a marriage, to*** *wake up every day, to work on their self-care instead of working on the care of their spouse.* No one can make us happy, nor can we make anyone happy. We must believe we are worthy and important and take the best care of ourselves. How we feel inside is the cake. How others may feel about us is icing on the cake. *When two married individuals take responsibility for their own self-worth and happiness, it becomes a set up for a very happy marriage.*

MARRIAGE AND INTERPOLATION

In the second chapter, we see that we interpolate. This means *we make an educated guess now about our lives, based on previous experiences, that felt like fact from childhood.* In other words, if a little boy grows up with a dad who plays and wrestles with him one minute and then out of nowhere is angry at him the next minute, he will have much trouble when he gets married. He will interpolate, or gauge based on his experience how things are going in his marriage. When the little boy grows up and gets married, he will have fun with his wife one minute and will expect something bad to happen the next minute. This will cause him not to want to connect with her. If he does connect with her, he could become afraid she will turn on him at any moment.

If a little girl is critiqued by her mother her whole life, when she marries, she may not even want to simply cook in fear of being criticized. If she decides to cook, she could be anxiously waiting for her husband not to like her cooking and criticize her. Dinner time could be a source of anxiety for her.

Both husband and wife come to the marriage seeing through a negative lens called their negative theme. They both interpolate and make an educated guess at what is going on in the marriage based on their past experiences. The tool for this is to share with their spouse what they are thinking and check it out.

Checking it out is a very simple process where instead of reacting to our automatic thoughts, we name our thoughts and see if our thoughts are accurate. A good example of *checking it out* was a time when I practiced it on my mother. My first counseling internship began doing trauma work at a hospital. The experience was so stressful that I would often go home and process some of the horrific content with my mother. My mom responded to me by giving me suggestions of how to help the victims. I really just wanted someone to listen because my experience seeing patients who were hurt or died was very taxing. Being involved in medical trauma, on the scene, was not my cup of tea.

As I processed the events, my mom gave me suggestions and then I automatically thought, *"She must not think I am helping the people very well."* Instead of thinking this, feeling it, and getting bitter, I simply *checked it out.* I said, *"Mom you have given me many suggestions about how to help the people experiencing*

trauma and I'm guessing it is because you think I am an

inadequate counselor. Is what I am thinking accurate?"

Much to my surprise she said, *"No honey, you are a natu-*

ral good counselor just like your father, however, if some

of my suggestions help you, then I can help them too!"

My automatic thoughts were entirely wrong.

Interpolation makes us an ***idiot*** and can definitely

leave us ***handicapped*** in our relationships. ***When you are***

unclear about what someone is saying, check it out! This

is the exact way to check out the messages in your mar-

riage-just ask.

MARRIAGE AND REACTION

Again, the word ***reaction*** means *"from"* not *"to."* On

the fourth of July, when someone lights a firework, it

looks like it is *to* the sky but it's actually *from* a device on

the ground. When someone shakes a bottle of soda and

opens it, it looks like it goes *to* the desk on the papers and *to* the floor, but in fact, it came *from* the bottle. When someone reacts, it undoubtedly can affect us, however, the meaning behind a person reacting is *about* the person who is reacting. The person is defending a negative feeling about him or herself. *When your spouse reacts, it is about your spouse; when you react, it is about you.*

We teach couples to take responsibility for their reactions. *If everyone took responsibility for his or her happiness, their feelings, and their actions, the world would be a different place.*

THE CAROUSEL RIDE

This is one of the most important paragraphs in this book. Pay very close attention because understanding this could change your life.

We will use Bill and Sally to explain the cycle in marriages. Bill had been very nice to Sally and could not get her attention. He had been ignored his whole life and now, once again, he was ignored. One day, after Bill had enough of being ignored, he began to curse at Sally. Sally thought Bill didn't love her and she felt worthless. Look at the direction of the arrows on the chart on pg. 89. Bill felt *unimportant* first then he reacted to that and cursed at her. What this means is Bill felt unimportant and his re-action of cursing was defending the unimportant feeling he had of himself. He didn't curse at Sally because he hated her. He cursed at Sally because he felt unimportant.

Then, Sally felt *inadequate* and ignored Bill even more. Her reaction of ignoring was defending her inade-quate feeling of herself. This is the continual cycle that goes 'round and round' for every couple. It is the cycle of blame and defense. One person reacts then the other per-son reacts. One person blames then the other person defends. ***The person who originally reacts is defending a feeling about himself/herself verses giving a message to the person.*** In time, both Bill and Sally realized what their reactions meant and saw the whole marriage through a different lens.

Whoever is reacting is defending a feeling about himself. Even in the most extreme examples of violence, the people who were violent did not hate the spouse they were being violent to. They were in fact reacting to their own shame and fear and their own self-hatred. In most cases, they were petrified their spouses would leave them and deep down inside felt unworthy of love. We will discuss what to do with this ineffective cycle regarding how couples communicate.

"THE CAROUSEL RIDE" CHART

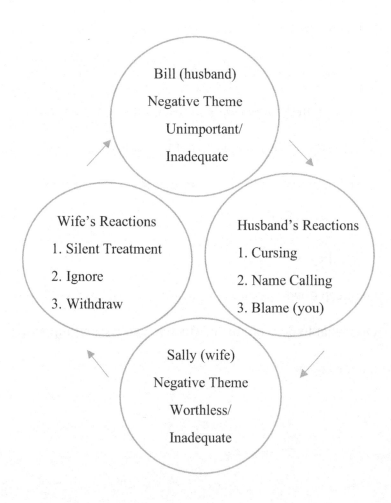

Bill (husband)

Negative Theme

Unimportant/

Inadequate

Wife's Reactions

1. Silent Treatment

2. Ignore

3. Withdraw

Husband's Reactions

1. Cursing

2. Name Calling

3. Blame (you)

Sally (wife)

Negative Theme

Worthless/

Inadequate

COMMON REACTIONS

- ❖ yell: to raise one's voice to get a point across

- ❖ ignore: to pay no attention to the subject or person

- ❖ curse: to use profane language

- ❖ withdraw: to retreat or isolate from another person

- ❖ joke: to use humor to distract

- ❖ sarcasm: to give a hidden message in a sarcastic manner

- ❖ run: to leave with intent of not dealing with the subject

- ❖ silent treatment: to not speak at all

- ❖ violence: to physically abuse a person

- ❖ preaching/lecture: to tell a person how to behave or act

- ❖ belittle: to use words to put a person down

- ❖ blame: to begin a statement with the word *"you"*

- ❖ defend: to continually explain why

- ❖ crazy make: to make a person believe they are crazy

- ❖ derail: to throw someone from one subject on to another

- ❖ name calling: to call someone a negative name

- ❖ label: to use a name with intent to put a person down

- ❖ lie: to tell the opposite of the truth

- ❖ cheat: to be unfaithful; infidelity

- ❖ addiction: the inability to say "no" to substances

Much of my career, I heard people say they were married to a manipulator. Manipulation is a method, in which we react, in hopes of manifesting an outcome. When we react, instead of responding to how we are really feeling, we are not dealing with truth. Let's look at a few examples of how we react and how we manipulate.

REACTION AND MANIPULATION

- ❖ yell: *I yell so she will do what I want.*
- ❖ ignore: *If I ignore him, he will listen.*
- ❖ people pleasing: *If I am nicer, he will be nicer.*
- ❖ silent treatment: *I'll show him and then he won't want to do that again.*
- ❖ violence: *When I threaten or get violent, she becomes afraid of me and won't leave me.*
- ❖ lecture: *As long as I tell her what to do, maybe she will not see what I'm doing.*
- ❖ belittle: *The more insecure she is, she won't have the courage to leave me.*

These are real examples, of what I have heard people say, for the reasons they react. Each and every one of us manipulate, whether we do it by people pleasing or being violent. When we react, we are defending a feeling about ourselves. ***Reacting never gives us what we want***. If we

91

are yelling because we have a need, we just get yelled back at. If we criticize because our needs are not met, we just receive criticism back. This is a cycle that occurs between two people, going nowhere. There is an answer of how to stop riding the Carousel *Ride* and move in forward motion.

STEPS TO EFFECTIVE COMMUNICATION

If I feel something negative, I must take responsibility for how I feel instead of blaming others. To be authentic about how I feel, ***I must use the word-"I."*** I must never use the word "you.*"* When we use the word "you," we are simply stating our opinion-and we all have one. Saying that, ***"I feel"*** a certain way and saying what ***"I need"*** gets me off of the carousel ride, that goes nowhere, and puts me in the direction of effective communication.

THE PERSON WITH THE NEED: COMMUNICATE

1. Identify how I feel and accept it.

2. Speak the truth with love by saying: "I feel _____ and I need _____."

The Effective way: *"I feel unimportant and I need time with you."*

The Ineffective way: *"You are a bad husband. You work nonstop and never spend time with me."*

THE PERSON RECEIVING THE NEED: LISTEN

1. Validate what you heard as if you are looking in a mirror.

Example: *"Wife, I understand you feel unimportant and need time with me."*

*We do not have to agree or even understand our spouse. We need to listen to our spouse and validate our spouse's feelings.

*Being heard is what most people want.

TAKING RESPONSIBILITY

When a person is reacting and not using healthy communication, we must create a boundary to stop the reaction. We must always use *I statements* and never use *you,* statements.

I can't do _____ (the persons reactions); however, I can do _____ (the behavior I would like to see).

> ➢ *I can't do screaming; however, I can do softer words.*

> ➢ *I can't do yelling; however, if you want to tell me how you feel, I will listen.*

> ➢ *I can't do silent treatments; however, when you are ready to talk, I'll listen.*

> ➢ *I can't do blame; however, I would be happy to hear how you feel.*

> ➢ *I can't do condescending remarks; however, I'd like to know what you need.*

> ➢ *I can't do belittling; however, I can listen if we can speak kinder words.*

To change the *handicaps* of marriage cycles that go nowhere, we must take responsibility for how we feel, our reactions, and discontinue the carousel ride of blaming our spouse and being defensive. We must take responsibility for ourselves by using "I" statements and take responsibility for how *we are allowing* others to treat us. Following this strategy can enrich both your marriage and other relationships.

While healthy communication is essential to successful marriages, sometimes marriages have much deeper issues. Often couples can be plagued by addiction and codependency. The next chapter will reveal what addiction and codependency are and will uncover tools of what to do with these debilitating symptoms that even the best of communication on earth could never resolve. The core of you is changing now getting you further and faster to realizing dreams.

Chapter 6-The Cycle of Addiction and

Codependency

Addiction is a ***brain disease.*** While all of us have had our challenges, having the ***handi-cap*** of the *brain disease* of addiction is one of the saddest, *deadly* diseases known to man. Addiction often leads to institutions, jail and death. While addiction can certainly make us look like an ***idiot,*** no one wakes up when they are little and says, *"When I grow up, I'd like to be a drug addict."* Substances have become a problem when an addict's life has become unmanageable.

Most people do not understand addiction, and many will judge those who are addicted. However, a lot of addicts are very intelligent, sensitive, deeply emotional, and intuitive people. And some addicts are known for having a sixth sense. Rest assured, there are answers to this *handicap* just like all the others. We see that humans afflicted with addiction are treatable and curable *one day at a time,* and in fact, become the most productive members of any country and any culture by getting help from a recovery program that works.

Codependency is a ***helping*** disease. While all of us have our challenges, the ***handicap*** of codependency is one of the most *destructive* diseases to the self-esteem. Codependents live through the challenges of helping other people. They are addicted to not only monitoring how people behave, but also how other people feel about them. The life of a codependent becomes unmanageable when the person become obsessed with controlling others, especially those with the brain disease of addiction.

Codependents are always taking care of the needs of others, but lack care for themselves. Codependents can be some of the most nurturing, compassionate, sensitive, caring people on the face of the earth. While codependency can definitely make an *idiot* of us all, we can all recover by getting involved in a recovery program that works.

LIBERTY UNIVERSITY TOWN HALL

My husband Dr. Richard Amato, founder of the *War on Addiction*, has spoken to over a million young people around the world. Recently, he was afforded an opportunity along with the First Lady, Melania Trump to address the opiate crisis to nine thousand people at Liberty University. ***Jerry Falwell, Jr., the President of Liberty University has now led the school to become the largest nonprofit University in the world and recently hosted a town hall meeting on the opiate crisis.***

Dr. Richard, an expert on the *brain disease* of addiction, spoke under the highest authority, privilege, and duty under the rule of law in our species. He spoke as a citizen of the United States of America. After explaining

that many people are predisposed to the *brain disease* of

addiction, his message was very clear. There is only one

war going on and it is the war on addiction. Dr. Richard

Amato's speech included the following messages. He said

to the young people gathered there about their generation,

"You do have a serious problem. And it will make you

the greatest generation that's ever lived or the last one."

He told them the statistics had shown that deaths had dou-

bled in the last six months, campaigning so hard for *hope*

not *handcuffs*.

Dr. Richard reminded them that statistics have

shown one hundred and seventy-five people are dying a

day and then he cried, ***"You want to find anguish, you***

want to find sorrow, you want to find financial expendi-

tures that are beyond belief, you want to find depression

and anxiety and suffering? Find an addict and follow

him home. Think pain." He explained because the human

brain, continues to develop from birth to age twenty-six–a process called neuroplasticity, young people are at risk when taking substances. He stated, *"Addiction cannot be cured, only managed."* He told the young people they have the power to choose, but they do not have the power to choose the consequence of their choices. He proceeded to say, *"No amount of prestige can save you from addiction."* Dr. Richard ended by saying, *"Once you are a pickle, you cannot be a cucumber again."*

The First Lady of the United States of America, Melania Trump, spoke next with passion saying, we need to remove the stigma of shame that comes with being an addict and instead take responsibility. Mrs. Trump said, *"I have learned that many people who become addicted to drugs are too ashamed to ask for help. I have also learned that addiction is a disease. And like any illness, people need and deserve treatment. We must commit to removing the stigma of shame that comes with addiction and helping change*

100

public opinion so that people find evidence-based treat-ment before it is too late. I have learned that you have a responsibility to yourself, and also to those around you who may be struggling. While you may never personally become addicted, the chances of you knowing someone who struggles with it are very high. And if you, or someone you know needs help, you need to be brave enough to ask, or strong enough to stand with them as they fight through the disease. You need to be educated enough to know the signs of addiction, and also secure enough to talk about it, and keep talking about it until help arrives." [5]

The handicap of addiction is affecting our families, marriages and homes in an astronomical way. Many people are embarrassed, regarding the truth of what is going on in their homes and find it difficult to get help. Having undealt with addiction in a family will not result in realized dreams. Addicts and those who love them must face the truth and confront the brain disease of addiction.

ADDICTION AND THE BRAIN

Many of us are naturally prone to look at an addict and

say, *"Wow he doesn't care about his family,"* and *"what*

a loser," or *"she's so irresponsible."* These words are

hurtful and show that most people do not understand what

happens with the brain disease of addiction. Addiction handicaps so many including robbing young people of their destiny.

Alcoholics Anonymous considers addiction an allergy of the body and an obsession of the mind.[6] Addiction means a person cannot say *no* and many of us will never understand what that is like. Imagine if you were a robot. Imagine if someone was in the driver's seat of your life telling you what to do. This is what addiction does; it treats the person as if they are a robot. It treats them as if something else is in control of them.

Our brain is made up of sections we call colonies; they are units of light. An example of a colony may be the section of mobility. This section of the brain moves your limbs automatically, without you specifically thinking about it. If you're able to walk and move easily, your mobility section is in sync with your limbs. Another example is the section of reasoning. This section helps us make good, rational and responsible decisions. The colonies of light have been seen on an MRI.

My husband, Dr. Richard Amato learned, from recent studies at the National Institute of Health, that when a person starts consuming alcohol or drugs, a new colony is created. The colony was not there before the consumption of the substance. The colony grows, and the more the substance is used, the more powerful the colony becomes. When the colony lights up, the individual experiences craving. Anything and everything can cause this colony to light up. It could range from having a memory of a trauma to just listening to rock-n-roll. When this colony lights up, the craving begins for the substance and the person can no longer say, *"No."* This is called addiction. This colony takes over the person to the point they can no longer choose what is good and rational. The more a person abuses substance the more it leads to changes in the structure and functioning of the brain. Addiction is progressive and chronic.

This is how a person with addiction issues becomes a living robot. The addiction colony and the reasoning colony are in war with each other. This is why addiction issues must be taken very seriously. Getting clean is not a 30-day war in rehab, but it is more likely a two-year war to get the colony in a desensitized less powerful state, eliminating cravings, coupled with maintenance, with a daily reprieve of the person's spiritual condition.

Like any other disease, once a person knows they have it, they must take responsibility for the cure. The only program for alcoholism, clinically proven through research to be effective in treating addiction, is *Alcoholics Anonymous.* This is a fellowship of men and women who share their experience, strength and hope with each other, so they may solve their common problem and help others to recover from **alcoholism.**

CODEPENDENCY AND ADDICTION

Codependency is an addiction, more hidden to the common man which can be equally as challenging as addiction. Many of us have this *helping disease* and do not know it. One of the largest challenges is that most spouses and families of addicts do not understand the addict is suffering with a brain disease. The person in a close relationship trying to help the addict is the *codependent*.

Imagine a codependent wife who is dealing with a drug addicted husband. She is unaware they are similar. While the addict is chasing the substance, the co-addict, the person who is codependent, is chasing the addict. ***The codependent needs the addict to need them.*** Being needed becomes her drug. The codependent spends copious hours, months, and even years enabling the addict by helping him, rescuing him and depending on her effectiveness at rescuing the addict for her self-worth.

In the end, the codependent is left chasing someone that can never fulfill her. She is left *waiting* for the addict to change, sometimes for a lifetime. She thinks the addict changing will make her happy. This never happens. She is typically left feeling resentful, mistreated, and angry. *Many codependents wake up years later to see they have wasted a lifetime taking care of an addict, to be left empty with nothing, and feeling all alone.* Just like the addict, the codependent feels that she is unable to break free from chasing her drug without help. Being aware of the drug-*the need to be needed* is the first step in getting help.

The codependent has a huge benefit or reward helping an addict. She *does not have to look at herself.* This person would rather be distracted than to feel the pain inside. This is why she is addicted to helping the addict. While having the pain of low self-esteem, she believes she is only worthy because she is a *"doing"* person instead of a *"being"* person. In other words, a codependent person only feels she has worth because of what she can do for others. Helping an addict gives her a *false sense* of self-worth. Eventually this person will exhaust herself and feel hopeless.

The **handicap** of the codependent is severe and creates a delusion. A parallel thought would be, *if I help a person with the disease of cancer get better, he will then see me as worthy of being loved* when, in fact, no one can cure the disease. No one can save an addict; he must save himself. Only having the gift of desperation and admitting defeat can save him. The codependent must admit defeat also; she cannot save the addict. Once a codependent realizes her life is unmanageable, she can give up and make a change.

Penny Amato Richardson, a recovering codependent says, ***"You can always go down one road and see what it is like. If you don't like it, you can do a U-turn and go*** *down a different road.*" Al-Anon (which is a group for those who have an addict they love), codependency groups, and licensed professional counseling are great ways to help a codependent get the help they need.

The entire family will need to get help for addiction and codependency. It is a cycle that can make an ***idiot*** of us all, much like the cycle of a *dog chasing its tail*. It is imperative that the addict, the co-addict, and the family of the addict all get the help that they need from the brain disease of addiction and the helping disease of codependency. It is essential each one learn to sit in their own skin, to realize they are an individual person, with a specific design, for a greater purpose. If you are an addict, take responsibility and do what you need to do for yourself. If you are a codependent, stop taking care of the responsibility of others and take care of yourself.

THE PRICE OF BEING KIND

Many people mistake codependency for *being kind*. I heard my whole life from my father, *"Always be kind."* The problem with this statement was that I believed it to be something it wasn't. Unfortunately, at times in my life I considered myself the *queen of codependency*. My life was spent being *nice* to people, not *kind.* I'm sure you have met the people who give everyone the benefit of the doubt, consider everyone's feelings more important than their own, and rarely argue because they crave peace. Half of my life was spent like this. This type of thinking left me compromised in my relationships, resentful, angry, burned out, with many regrets. I realized everyone's feelings and needs had mattered except mine. Plagued by codependency, I had to learn the hard way. While my dad was right, **"Always be kind,"** kind did not mean what I thought it did.

According to Merriam Webster, the word *kind* is a group united by common traits.[7] This would be like a group of individuals or instances sharing common traits. Kindness reflects a trait which reflects truth. When we decide to *people please,* it is not love if it is not the truth. The most loving and kind thing we can do for another person is to be real by reflecting the truth. That is *kind.* Telling people what they want to hear and doing things for others, that we don't really want to do, is living a lie and is not kind.

Think about it like this, ***being nice is for those who are scared of conflict. It has nothing to do with spirituality. REAL KINDNESS is about being honest with ourselves and others. If we want to be authentic, we must live truth. Truth will lead us down the road of setting safe boundaries for ourselves, in our relationships with others. This will lead us to an everlasting freedom that being nice can't give.*** When I think of my dad's saying, *"Always be kind,"* I think *do yourself and others a favor by speaking the truth with love.* This is the ultimate *kindness* that can save us from living years of unfulfilled dreams. And this is how we can truly love ourselves.

RELIGIOUS ADDICTION

This is an addiction that is often a surprise to many. Religious addiction is an obsessive compulsivity with rituals, rights and the performance of certain symbolic and emotional tasks. This is where a person is performance-based, and their self-worth is wrapped up in doing the right thing, being good, obeying laws or seeing to it that those they interact with are doing the right thing also. In contrast, spirituality is a heartfelt, spontaneous manifestations of emotions motivated by a genuine concern for others. A spiritual person lives in an existential state of authenticity, caring for the packaged health of themselves and others.

Religious addicts often spend their time thinking or talking about the performance of others. The drug for the religious addict is obsessing about the behavior of others. They act out ritualistic behaviors to fulfill their obsession. This could be a phone call to gossip or even pray for someone. Some ritualistic behavior may come through preaching or confrontation, regarding the person that they are evaluating.

Examples of religious addiction would be the people who enjoy discussion of the businessman who had an affair with his secretary, the alcoholic neighbor next door, their cousins latest divorce, or their co-worker's pregnant daughter. Discussion of such matters are primarily used to make themselves feel better, by having a similar reward to the codependent, distracting them from themselves. Many *do-gooder,* religious addicts are looked at by others as judgmental. When some are judgmental, most of the time, they are simply trying to escape the pain they feel.

Concentrating on other people's sins, bad choices or hardships can definitely serve as a **handicap** to those who would like to be healthy, productive members of society.

In contrast, genuine spirituality is when we look at ourselves and our spiritual condition. When we take care of ourselves first, we may be in a healthy position to help others. Genuine spirituality is when a conflict happens, and we ask ourselves the question, *"What is my part in this?"* Genuine spirituality will ask, *"How may I serve?"*

Religious addicts are not bad people. They are people who are full of fear and shame with a genuine deep-seated thought, *"If people knew who I really was they wouldn't like me."* Sometimes these people are the most afraid of God. Their idea of God is often a person waiting to beat them with a club, as soon as they do something wrong. Religious addicts need licensed professional help also. Anyone who is trying to escape themselves, by changing another person, needs to get the help that they deserve. No one can be perfect. We all have flaws. There is nothing a person can do and no task they can perform to give them worth or acceptance, especially to God. We all have worth because of who we are.

WHAT ALL ADDICTIONS HAVE IN COMMON

Precipitating trauma: Normally from childhood, we have unresolved trauma that precedes our addictions to substance, helping people, or religion. We have unmet needs where we use the addiction to substances, people and religion to *escape* ourselves and find comfort and control. When a person faces unresolved trauma from childhood when they are older, the onset of addiction can happen in adulthood. When we escape ourselves, we are seeking comfort from connection to someone or something and finding a sense of power and control. This creates a repetitive cycle, sometimes continued for the rest of a person's life.

The addictive cycle: Obsessive thinking occurs first about the substance, person, or performance of self or others. Next, a repetitive behavior is acted out (using the substance, helping the addict, or gossiping about someone) and then the person feels shame. The person becomes addicted to the shame as they repeat the never-ending cycle.

A. The addict feels shame when they cannot stop drinking and abusing drugs.
B. The codependent feels shame when they cannot fix the addict and they feel unloved.
C. The religious addict feels shame because they can never be perfect.

The similar beliefs: All those with addiction seem to believe the following:

A. I am bad.
B. No one truly cares for me.
C. My dreams will never come true.
D. My greatest need is my drug. (substance, helping people, being perfect)

Taking responsibility is no easy task. If we were to tragically get in a car accident, hit by a drunk driver on our nearest big highway, it would in no way be our fault. If our leg was broken in the accident, we would have to go in the ambulance, go under potential surgery, and continue on with weeks, if not months, of physical therapy. Although the accident was not our fault, we would have to take responsibility for what happened to us. Often in life, we experience trauma that precedes the different types of addictive behaviors we have begun.

We can use that trauma as an excuse for the reasons we continue to stay sick. When we begin to accept, we may have an addiction, whether it is to substances, helping people, or perfecting others and ourselves, we need to get rid of the shame tied to our addictions and take responsibility by getting licensed professional help. What happened to us is not our fault, however, we must take responsibility. Addiction must be taken seriously and dealt with above anything else. If you need professional help *call 1-855-SET-FREE*.

Addiction to substances, people, and performance all distract us from ourselves. It makes an *idiot* of us all and *handicaps* us from becoming free of ourselves and others to be the happiest, most productive members of society. We run from ourselves so long we do not realize our dreams. While some of the saddest stories of my practice included those dealing with addiction, I have seen the greatest miracles when an addict decides to get help. Facing addiction will prove rewarding results. The next few chapters will give Light and understanding to where the power comes from to dream, believe, and finally achieve what you have so long waited for.

Chapter 7-The Conditioning of Dreams

Many of us act a *part* much like those acting on television our entire lives because of the way we were conditioned. When we perform, we behave in a particular way for another group of people. The reason so many of us perform is because we consider our real self-*unacceptable* and stamp ourselves *unworth*y. We were conditioned to see and believe a certain way about ourselves, and therefore, left in shortage of satisfying our dreams.

If a child is told they are good, they will often follow what others tell them to do even to their own detriment. If a child is told they are bad, most likely, they will be bad. Many of us are conditioned to expect less and complete what others want, therefore, leaving us with a *handicap*. Many of us have lived a *false self* for other people. ***The key to recondition ourselves for realized dreams is to find out who we truly are; we must seek to find our real self.***

The fear of intimacy can be a big indicator that we don't have *self-acceptance*. We fear for people *to know* us because deep down inside we believe we are unworthy and unlovable. We escape this fear by performing. We march on with how we were conditioned as children and dare not dream and believe in who we really are and what we really want. One of the ways we can evaluate *self-acceptance* is to evaluate *self-dislike*. When we dislike ourselves, we can take on a lifestyle of punishing ourselves.

INDICATORS OF DISLIKE AND PUNISHMENT

➢ Staying in an abusive marriage

➢ Working with abusive people

➢ Calling yourself names

➢ Constantly saying you're sorry

➢ Allowing yourself to be bullied

➢ Bullying another person

➢ Pretending a lifestyle

➢ Staying in an unsatisfying career

➢ Overeating/undereating

➢ Binging and purging

➢ Substance abuse

➢ Laziness or lack of exercise

➢ Financial enslavement

➢ Constantly running late

➢ Allowing others to take care of you

➢ Pleasing others

➢ The need to be needed

➢ Taking care of others

THE PROCESS OF SELF-TALK

The past brought us a major undersupply of satisfaction, as we performed and lived punishing ourselves, for being unworthy. Now we must take on *self-care* of the mind, by nurturing ourselves daily, through a process of identifying and monitoring our *self-talk*. This will put us on a path of manifesting a life we have never lived.

Before we can see our dreams realized, we need to take the time to see what is going on inside of us by identifying our *automatic thoughts.* An automatic thought is a thought we do not have to think about. It is when someone walks in the room and our thoughts automatically say something. The next time you accidentally drop your phone, identify your automatic thought. Did you say, *"You are an idiot"* or did you say, *"it's okay?"* The influence we can have on ourselves by monitoring our automatic thoughts is astronomical. We may be speaking to ourselves in such a way that is *self-promoting* or *self-*

denoting. Once we identify what our automatic thoughts are saying, we need to talk back to those thoughts in a way that promotes *self-acceptance.* This is called *self-talk.*

SELF-TALK THAT MATCHES DREAMS

Get out a journal and spend the next day or even week tracking and writing down your *automatic thoughts.* Write down what you say about yourself and how you feel about yourself. Write down what you believe others are thinking of you and how you feel in relationship with them. Do you speak in a way that is promoting self-acceptance and giving confidence to your dreams being realized? Or are you speaking to yourself in self-contempt? Perhaps you are your greatest fan; perhaps you are your worst enemy. *Make sure your self-talk matches the dreams you have.*

When you find you are bullying yourself, use *self-talk* to dispute that. Be kind to yourself. Great power lives in what we tell ourselves. We have the power to tear ourselves down or build ourselves up. We have the power to destroy and the power to heal and triumph!

Next, in your journal write what you like about yourself. Once we identify the automatic thoughts and evaluate how we speak to ourselves, we can change our thoughts to reflect the truth; thus, we begin the transformation process. *It is through the transformation of the mind that our dreams come true.*

THE KEY TO REALIZED DREAMS

Deep down inside, we all have dreams. Some of us know what they are and some of us do not. Many of us worry that our dreams will never come true. Others have dared *"to dream,"* like the familiar song by Aerosmith says, '*Dream on, dream on, dream it till your dreams come true,*' yet have seen no results. [8]

While *"to believe"* may change the chemicals in the brain, the part missing in dreams being realized is the transformation process. We must not only dream but learn. Dreams don't manifest until the mind is transformed. **To dream, to believe, and to be transformed equals realized dreams. Dreams will come true and will be bigger than you have imagined.**

THE SUBCONSCIOUS AND THE CONSCIOUS

Our mind is made up of two parts; the subconscious and the conscious. The subconscious mind is where our beliefs and perceptions are stored. This is what we covered in the six previous chapters. Our conscious mind is where we have thoughts and make decisions. This is what we are looking at today. It is imperative that we uncover the way we were conditioned. We must get in touch with our subconscious mind to be able to recondition ourselves and make conscious decisions.

To change any addictive cycle, like that of alcoholics, we must consider a daily reprieve, by examining our thoughts and the ways in which we speak to ourselves. Changing both the subconscious beliefs as well as conscious thoughts is essential to the transformation process. According to dictionary.com 'transformation' means a change in form, appearance, nature, or character.[9]

THE PROCESS OF TRANSFORMATION

Just like the caterpillar changed *form* when he stopped eating, hung upside down, spun in a cocoon, and waited until he emerged as a butterfly, we must stop and undergo the process of becoming our new self. What happens during the *waiting time* in a cocoon is fascinating. The old body is broken down and then it turns into something new. The process a caterpillar must undertake, to *appear* as a beautiful butterfly, is the same one we need to take. We must get rid of the way we were conditioned and become a new person-a *genuine* person.

While the inside of us changes, the outside of us will naturally change also. We were born with traits, skills, and a purpose reflecting our nature. The very process of being transformed was meant to be. The **character** traits of the butterfly seem vastly different from that of the caterpillar. Like the butterfly, when our minds transform, we can change so much that we are not even recognizable.

THE BENEFIT OF PRESSURE

If a butterfly comes out of the cocoon *too early,* it is able to pollinate the flowers one time, and then it loses strength and dies. It does not live as the beautiful butterfly was meant to live. It must come to complete transformation to have the strength to stay alive and fulfill its purpose.

To create a perfect insect, a moth has to force its way through the neck of a cocoon with hours and hours of intense struggle. The pressure is what gives life to his wings. If he does not undergo the *pressure* and comes out too early, his wings will not be developed, and he will die.

Just like these insects, we must go through the transformation process to see our dreams come true. We must undergo pressure as well. It is okay to have gratitude for your hardships. If we don't undergo pressure, we will not be strong enough for what is to come.

Having your dreams come true does not come from a rainbow with a leprechaun at the end of it waiting to hand you a pot of gold, just as much as babies do not come hand delivered by storks. Having your dreams come true requires a lot of work. The transformation process can be very stressful.

Sometimes we try to lessen the pressure for others or ourselves. The times when we attempt to lessen the pressure for others, we enable them to be weak. ***When we enable people, it is like cutting the moth out of the cocoon too early and setting him up to die as he will have no strength of his own to fly***. This is why it is important for us to allow others to go through their transformation process, as it is equally as important, we go through ours. Every individual person must go through their own transformation process. Transformation will not come by another person changing; transformation comes when *you* change.

THE BENEFIT OF STORMS

More often than not, the trauma we experience can cause us to give up on the transformation process. The storms we have been through may have been gut-wrenching, mind blowing, and have defeated us. These storms, even though we do not understand them, are putting the pressure on us to bring us to where we need to be.

Through the storms, we grow. When a lightning storm appears, we can become afraid. The wind blows, the lightning crashes and it can bring much damage. The other side of a lightning storm brings something we cannot see. There is nitrogen in the air and when lightning crashes, it forces that nitrogen into the ground, and this is what makes our crops and flowers grow. It is the storm that produces growth. It is the storm that gives us daily food, and it is the storm that makes the flowers pretty.

CHANGE IS NECESSARY

Sometimes we may have to change our thinking in small steps to allow for a behavioral change. If a person wants to lose weight, they not only have to go to the gym, change their food intake, and possibly get a nutritionist to help them, but they will have to use *self-talk* to get themselves out of bed. They will have to use *self-talk* to get themselves in the car and *self-talk* to drive to the gym. They need to use *self-talk* to go back one day at a time until their body is transformed.

If you are depressed and suicidal, you may have to use *self-talk* to change the thoughts you have of putting yourself down. If you dream to have a loving husband and you have one who is beating you, you may have to make a *behavioral change* before you may have a good husband. The transformation process is a minute by minute, day by day endeavor where we identify our *automatic thoughts* and change our *self-talk*. Then we make a decision to match our thoughts to who we really are, what we are dreaming for, and finally choose to do the next right thing.

THE PROCESS OF SELF-ACCEPTANCE

Take your journal and write a list of thoughts you have of yourself. Which ones do you believe are true? Which ones do you believe are lies? Take the lies you believe and write out disputes for them, and then write out replacements for those lies.

As we weed out the lies of how we were conditioned as children, we will throw *self-dislike* in the trashcan and will come to *self-acceptance*. This is how we will no longer accept being an *idiot* who is living with an unnecessary *handicap*. The more our minds are transformed through this process, the more we will identify our genuine self. Your inventor made a *showpiece* when he made you, certainly a piece worth revealing. In the next chapter we will take the next step of uncovering the new real you!

Chapter 8-Reconditioning
My true authentic self

The two greatest needs of any human are to love and be loved. Some of us look our entire lives for love. Like the familiar song by Johnny Lee says, *"Looking for love in all the wrong places."*[10] The desire to love and be loved is hardwired in the brain. We all need to belong to someone; even our animal instinct says we should belong in a pack. Being loved meets our needs of safety and security.

When others love us, we feel accepted, so we look to others so that we may accept ourselves. We need community with each other, so we can grow. The mystery has been revealed that we looked at life through the lens of our negative theme. In times past, this caused a great disconnect in how we viewed ourselves, how we thought others saw us, and how we thought God looked at us. Not understanding that we had worth and that we were worth loving made *idiots* of us all, leaving us hopeless with a *handicap*. Now we are free to love ourselves. We are free to discover authenticity and come to *self-actualization*. We are free to be who we were meant to be. ***Finding myself means finding my inventor and discovering the reason for which I exist. Dreams being actualized are very near.***

WHY DO PEOPLE INVENT?

Imagine the *thought* that went into inventing the first chair. The chair was invented with the purpose to sit upright so that we may sit in a room and be comfortable. In the past, people would sit on the floor. Inventors today constantly improve the comfort, shape, and design of chairs by making them look more appealing and feel more comfortable. When we look through a negative lens, we are not looking at ourselves accurately, therefore, we do not function the way we are meant to function. It would be like us telling the inventor of a chair we have decided to put the chair upside down and sit on the legs. It would not work, and it would not serve the purpose the inventor created the chair for.

Like the chair, we were invented with a purpose. When a person who is made of great worth, who has a fingerprint one out of eight billion *feels worthless,* he will not be able to function the way he was meant to function. The one who invented *YOU* made no other person exactly like you. The inventor proved by your DNA that a duplicate of you could not be found in any other country, state, city, or even down the road.

My sister Jennifer Drennan always says, *"**God made us all different. You are the best! Love and be yourself.**"* There are no words to describe your astronomical worth. ***You are the only you that will ever exist.*** To feel worthless would be like sitting in the upside-down chair; it does not work nor match the way we were made. Therefore, we must take full responsibility for the negative script we have received to recondition ourselves to believe the truth. At this point, *we may not yet know who we are; we just know we are worth finding out.* Who are we to say to the potter how to form the clay? Who are we to say to our inventor how we should function?

WHO INVENTED ME?

While I am not offering a particular religious belief in this section, I am asking that you open up your heart and mind to a new way of looking at things. When it comes to negative thoughts and themes of worthlessness, unimportance, and inadequacy, we projected our negative themes into the *I with the Higher Power* relationship. This concept has repeatedly revealed itself for years and years in my counseling practice. When we asked ourselves the question, *what do I think the Higher Power thinks of me,* we saw that an honest response matched our theme.

Simply put, when we believe we are unimportant, we assume the Higher Power feels the same way. This thought process has blocked our ability to love and be loved. We must remove this barrier, so life may flow easily like a peaceful river. We must see the Higher Power differently and open our hearts and minds to a new concept that it is time to accept love.

WHY DO WE INVENT?

When a woman decides to become pregnant, she so badly wants *to have a baby to love.* She wants to nurture, protect, and love her baby. Picking out a name for her baby is something she is very excited about. When the baby arrives, she loves to hold, hug, and kiss her baby. Mothers can be like my mother and be *a mother hen* or *a mother bear* when it comes to protecting her baby. Women are very proud of their children and love to show them off.

When a man decides to have a baby, he wants to leave a legacy with his baby. He wants to teach his baby everything he knows, coach his teams, and have his baby carry his name. A dad loves to play and provide for his baby. Dads love to brag also.

When a person wants to invent something, he has a very good reason; there is a purpose and a plan. Perhaps we were invented for a very good reason. One day, I Googled, *why did God make us?* The first article that popped up said, *"So He would have someone to love."* I pondered at length on this very profound thought.

This is challenging, but instead of looking at the Higher Power through our eyes let us try something new. For a little while, let us imagine the Higher Power as *the One who loves you and desires a personal relationship with you, so He has someone to love.* What if the entity that set the planets rotating perfectly in order really cares about your life? Imagine if the Higher Power felt like an asset verses a liability to hide from. *What if it's love?* What if the Higher Power really loves you? What would this mean?

IF IT'S LOVE...

If God loved us like a good parent loves a child, He may have dreamed us into existence. He may have decided what we should look like and made us perfect in His eyes. Most good parents see their children as beautiful, and most children look like their parents. He may have created us to look like Him, in His image. He most likely had a specific plan and purpose.

Most parents, even from when their child is in the womb dream of who their child may become. Perhaps God dreamed of who we would become. God must think more good thoughts of us than we could ever imagine. I do about my children. Don't you? Most parents at some point are *goo goo* over their children. I know I have been.

Parents discipline their children to keep them safe, I'd imagine God does too. Parents love to teach their children everything. He probably likes to teach us as well.

The responsibilities of parents are endless. Every good parent provides shelter, clothes and food for their children. And really good parents care about their children's feelings, by listening and validating them. When a child is sad, the parent will comfort them. When parents can help a child in any way, they do. Parents want kids to have fun and enjoy themselves.

Parents just smile when they look at their children because they are pleased. The child is their blood, their kin, and they are proud. I'm sure God is proud of us too. Parents want to lift the burdens of their children. Perhaps God cares to lift our burdens as well. At the end of the day, a good parent will lay their very life down for their child. If God made us *so He would have someone to love,* what extent would He go to as our parent?

THINK ABOUT THE FOLLOWING QUESTIONS

➢ Could the Higher Power have dreamed me into existence?

➢ Could the Higher Power have made me look a certain way?

➢ Could the Higher Power have made me in His Image?

➢ Could the Higher Power have a plan? A purpose?

➢ Could the Higher Power think good thoughts of me?

➢ Could the Higher Power try to teach me something?

➢ Could the Higher Power fulfill my desires and dreams?

➢ Could the Higher Power be pleased even though I am not perfect?

➢ Could the Higher Power comfort me?

➢ Could the Higher Power help me?

➢ Could the Higher Power heal me?

➢ Could the Higher Power provide for me?

➢ Could the Higher Power make me happy?

➢ Could the Higher Power die for me?

IF ITS LOVE... WHAT DOES IT

MEAN?

I have worth.

I have security.

I have my needs met.

I have purpose.

I have my burdens carried.

I have someone pleased with me.

I have someone who accepts me.

I have someone to depend on.

I have someone to ask for help.

I have confidence.

I have a friend.

I have comfort.

I have life.

I have love.

I have everything.

THE BELIEF THAT CHANGED MY LIFE
How could believing this change your life?

Imagine for one day that He made *YOU* so He would have someone to love. This belief could change your life also. The best book on who God is *as our parent* was written by Warren Marcus, ***"The Priestly Prayer of the Blessing."*** [11] Seek a Higher Power of your own understanding. It has been necessary for my mental health to believe there is a God and I am not Him. The facts show anything ever invented had an inventor; everything that was invented was made for a reason with a purpose.

Knowing *WHO* I truly am allows me to function *AS I SHOULD*. Believing anything different was counter-productive and left me with a *handicap*. I am full of gratitude and happiness knowing I was invented for such a time as this-to let you know that you have worth. To give love and receive love has brought me the greatest fulfillment. Ask yourself, *who am I, really*? *I AM!*

Chapter 9-Reconditioning
The Power of Faith

Nothing else in this life matters except faith working through love. Faith is an assured perception that is based on truth, not the constructs of a person's mind. Faith is revealed through belief, confidence, and *action*. To have something different, to get well, we have to do something different. If nothing changes, nothing changes.

My life did not change, and my dreams did not come true until I stepped out of my old script of believing the lies of negative messages and surrendered to faith. Once I had faith, I was **no longer an idiot,** doing the same things repeatedly; therefore, I was **no longer handicapped**, repeating the same cycles. Faith began when I decided that the Higher Power was, ***"The One who loves me and desires a personal relationship with me because***

He wants someone to love" verses the religious one of my script. My dependency on God consisted of the fact that I was not Him and I must turn my entire life over to the care of Him; and I did just that.

THE FAITH TO GO

After years of being in an abusive relationship that consisted of daily intellectual and emotional abuse, I had the first suicidal thought of my life. This was my indicator it was time to stop repeating negative cycles and get out of my marriage. The lesson I learned was that *it is my job to teach people how to treat me.*

There was nothing left for me to do but take responsibility for myself. **I went through a gut-wrenching divorce and became a single mother.** My three small children and I began a journey with God. My fear was indescribable, and I could not have made it, *"being a single mother,"* without making the decision that God was both my husband and me and the children's father. My credit cards became maxed out due to the lawyer fees from the divorce, and there was very little money to provide for them. The children and I left our home state of Maryland, with consent where I had been a licensed counselor, supervising twenty-one counselors. We temporarily went to the state of Michigan to study and learn non-profit work.

PAIN INTO PURPOSE

While we were in Michigan, I decided to become licensed in counseling because, due to court battles, I had to stay much longer than I had intended. For two years, Michigan became our home. The children and I had very little money and we prayed a lot. One time we had no food in the kitchen, no gas in the gas tank and had only twenty-five dollars to our name with credit cards maxed out and bills due. We decided to put ten dollars in the gas tank, buy ten dollars' worth of groceries for the four of us to eat and keep five dollars in the account to keep it open.

146

Much of the time we lived in Michigan money was very limited.

Michigan wasn't like Maryland where I held supervisory status and ran a private practice. The counseling requirements in Michigan were different, so I was only able to hold an intern status there until I received more hours to get a full license. My intern hours were spent working in community counseling where most of my clients had very little money and many of my clientele had substance abuse issues. Interestingly enough, this is where I found my passion to help addicts and the families of addiction. Eventually, I earned both my full counseling license and supervisory status for Michigan.

Michigan for me was a very hard season. The journey of change was long and taxing. When we step out in faith, there are many trials, and dreams do not happen overnight. At that point, I dreamed that providing for my kids to eat would become easier. The transformation process was stressful.

When a person changes the way they are living because it is unhealthy for them, they want things to feel better right away. Like many women who have been in compromising marriages, leaving meant economic insecurity. It was like trading one big problem for a smaller problem. Although it was hard, my first year in Michigan was the happiest I had felt in fifteen years. Although there were new struggles, what I learned in the process of becoming mentally healthy would prove to affect me positively for the rest of life and the rest of my career. For the first time in my life, I was poor, and then grew a heart for poor people and single mothers. My poor status caused me to depend on God more than ever. I had experiences with Him that I will never forget. ***Dr. Tim Clinton, the President of the American Association of Christian Counselors (AACC) says, "The more dependent you*** *become on God, the more independent you become in*

life."[12]

THE FAITHFUL PROVIDER

One month, I realized I was one thousand dollars short of my bills that were due in seven days. We had no cash and the credit cards were maxed due to the hefty costs of being sent to court over and over again. I prayed and said, *"God you are my Husband and you are our Father. You can afford us. I have calculated all the money coming from Maryland phone sessions and the Michigan counseling center and we will be one thousand dollars short in seven days. Please provide us with one thousand dollars in the next seven days."* This is an unbelievably true story. Within the next 24 hours, WITHOUT me telling anyone, three people called me asking if I needed money. I humbly said yes, and they sent checks in the mail that totaled nine hundred and seventy-five dollars which I received in the mail within seven days.

At first, I felt humiliated and embarrassed to receive money from others, until I saw the children cheering when they opened the mail at the mailbox. We stood amazed as we knew God truly cared for us and provided for us. He was the best Husband any woman could ever ask for and He was indeed the best Father. In a prayer of gratitude, with tears in my eyes, I said, *"Thank you! I can't believe you provided for us like that!"* Then I proceeded to say, *"I just opened the last bill of twenty-five dollars due to a hospital; it's okay we are only twenty-five dollars short of the one thousand. I'll pay them back next week. It's ok God. Thank you so much! You gave us nine hundred and seventy-five of the one thousand dollars I asked for!"* And what happened next, I will never forget.

I opened the last piece of mail, which I knew was a check for sixty dollars from a lady I did work with in Maryland. This money was already calculated as money coming for bills. I stood in astonishment as I opened up the card to see it was a check for eighty-five dollars. She wrote a check for twenty-five dollars more than she owed! The card said, *"Thank you for all your help, Susan. I am sending you an extra $25. God told me to give it to you."*

While my uncontrollable tears were flowing, my children were praising God. We received exactly one thousand dollars in seven days and every single bill we had got paid. I knew my children and I had the greatest love of all-The *Love of One who just wants someone to love.* **We knew we had the Love of a Husband and the Love of a Father.** There are countless stories like this where I now have proof and know-God truly loves us! The lack of money could never replace the priceless lessons we learned of faith.

A newfound respect for God was developed and my past reflected doing things my way never worked, so I really sought to know what my Higher Power wanted. My eyes were glued to Him every step of the way. *"Why was I made; For what reason did I exist?"* Before I was able to leave Michigan to return to Maryland, it became very apparent that we were not supposed to return to Maryland, as the road seemed to be leading somewhere else. There was a job offer in another state that was like the work I did in Maryland.

At first, I was very apprehensive of going until all the signs of the universe seemed to clearly point in that direction. I surrendered to the opportunity and got licensed in counseling in another state. With permission of the courts, the children and I decided to enter a journey of faith to sunnyside Florida, the *Promised Land.*

THE FAITH TO HEAL

The process to healing that we are afforded is much like the Israelites in the Old Testament. The journey to go from Egypt through the wilderness to the Promised Land was meant to be an eleven-day journey. Some had an opportunity to leave Egypt where they were slaves, go through the wilderness, and enter the Promised Land.

The symbol of Egypt reminds me of being comfortable with the childhood ways we were conditioned. When the going got tough, the Israelites begged their leader to go back to Egypt instead of facing their fear in the wilderness to get to a much better place.

Change is scary. I can validate that! Like the Israelites, we are often slaves with coping mechanisms we learned from the way we were raised. However, some wanted a change so much they opted to go through the wilderness and eventually went into the Promised Land. The wilderness, being much like the transformation process is where we grow.

The Promised Land is a place of rest. This is where we achieve acceptance of self and finally rest in the fact, we have indescribable worth and an intentional destiny for our lives. The Israelites who rejected their addictive cycles and surrendered to a Power greater than themselves entered the land flowing with milk and honey. The rest is history! Like some of the Israelites, intentional destiny is what I was seeking, and my eyes were on God.

THE FAITH TO FOLLOW DIRECTIONS

When we step out in faith, to do what we have never done to be reconditioned, it is scary. The day came where I gave notice to my clients in Michigan, gave notice to my apartment, sold my belongings, and made a decision to take the job, twenty-two hours away from where the children and I had been residing, and move to Florida. Things do not always go the way we imagine, and change is both a challenge and a process. It is the process that changes our core requiring much patience and a lot of time and work.

My last week was spent sitting in the empty apartment, waiting for the day to leave. A few days before I was supposed to leave, I received a phone call from the person who was supposed to hire me. They confessed they were suddenly leaving their place of employment and would therefore be unable to hire me. As I had already given up my job, housing and sold my furniture, I prayed about what to do and felt led to *go in faith.* I visited my hometown in Maryland for two weeks and then on my birthday, July 11, 2012, headed to the Promised Land.

Driving to Florida that day was one of the scariest days of my life. The children had visitation with their biological father for a few weeks, so I took our clothes with all the credit cards maxed out, only two thousand dollars cash to my name, no job, and drove eighteen hours from Maryland to Florida, not knowing where I would even lay my head that night. What did I have to lose?

My experience had proven God was real. That was no longer a question. He wanted someone to love. Well, I love Him, therefore, I am going to go where I believe He wants me to go. Still petrified with doubt that I could be the laughingstock of those who knew me, I proceeded on in faith. The truth was that I had the support of my mother-who is a *mother hen*, Eloise Drennan, and my sister Jennifer Drennan cheering me on. Like my sixteen-year-old daughter Megan says, ***"Live your best life! Don't care what anyone has to say about you."***

While driving alone in the car, trying to distract my nervousness with music, the phone rang. It was a lady who lived in Tennessee that I knew from childhood. She proceeded to say, *"I hear you are on your way to Florida. I'm visiting Boca Raton, Florida right now. Where are you staying tonight? I'll be here for three days. Come and stay with me."* Honestly, I was floored; it was as if I was in a dream. For the next three nights, I stayed on her air mattress. Every time I panicked about what would happen after the three days, I told myself, *"Don't worry about tomorrow. You are okay for today."*

THE MIRACLES OF FAITH

On day four, I received another phone call. There was a lady in Wellington, Florida whose husband was out of town for two weeks and I had an offer to stay with her until his return home. While staying at her house, I heard a message shoot through my head while I was standing under a palm tree. *"Wellington is where you can reside. It has the best schools for the children."* I knew nothing about the area. Sure enough, I looked up Wellington and it had the best rated schools in Palm Beach County.

After two weeks, another woman from Wellington said I could stay in her office for two weeks as it had a bed in it. In the meantime, I was developing a little bit of income enough to survive daily but not enough to pay rent for a month. Five days before my children arrived in

Florida, my brother Greg Drennan, out of nowhere called and said, *"Little sister, God told me to give you two thousand dollars or He will kill me."* My brother has never given me money in my entire life. I didn't ask for it. And, I certainly hope God would not have killed him, however, I gladly accepted his offer and my brother wired me two thousand dollars.

The first month's rent for a three-bedroom apartment in Wellington, Florida including deposits and fees totaled one thousand nine hundred and eighty dollars. From there, a person heard about us, donated some furniture, and I used my last seven hundred dollars cash and bought three mattresses. The money my brother sent was a *miracle* that got the children and I started in Florida.

The children were so happy to arrive at their new home in beautiful promised land, sunny side Florida. Once the first month's rent was paid, I had no idea how the second month would be paid. However, every single solitary month for the next four years, all the bills were paid. All three of my children and I know because of our experience that God is faithful. Years later, my son Michael emailed me from college and said, *"Mom you raised me to take turmoil face-first and trust in God."* To this day, he brags constantly of the faithfulness of God. All four of us were glad there was someone bigger and better than us that needed *someone to love*. What we experienced has impacted us for a lifetime.

FAITH TO FRUITION

We began our Florida non-profit called ***Dream, Believe...Transforming Lives Corporation***. This is where a person could undergo the transformation process of counseling to see their dreams come true. By calling **1-855-SET-FREE** anyone from Maryland, Virginia, Michigan, and Florida can call and get help. A percentage of the counseling fees go to give food, medicine, and Bibles to the poor and needy.

Everything about the name of the non-profit, the goal, and helping those in need all came by clear direction and leading from God. When things began taking off, my only hesitancy in establishing this work was the fact that a deep-seated personal dream of mine never came true. So, how was I to run the Dream Believe business? I proceeded to ask, *"I have seen so many people's dreams come true my whole career except mine. How can I run a Dream Believe business?"* Then I heard, *"They went to counseling and you didn't."*

From there, I listened again to the One who wants someone to love. The journey of inner transformation began when I entered counseling, codependent groups, and recovery work. The next couple years was hard work cleaning out and uncovering the real me. The old Susan with a script gained new thoughts and learned new ways. I was escaping the cycle going nowhere. Finally, I was going somewhere. My heart had opened up to a new concept of a Higher Power where I asked. Who am I re-

ally? And once I sought me, I found me.

Chapter 10-Reconditioning
Who am I?

When an inventor made a chair he said, *"Sit in it like this."* When an artist created a painting he said, *"Put it on the wall like this."* When a shoemaker made shoes he said, *"Put the shoe on like this."* When a person made a drinking straw they said, *"It is for drinking water like this."*

When we do not know *who we are* or *what we are,* we cannot know our primary purpose or function. Not knowing who we are can be much like a fish out of water, floundering about with no purpose. Not knowing who we are makes us an *idiot,* leaving us with unnecessary *handicaps,* causing us to be in all sorts of addictive cycles. **Just like anything else invented, we have a primary purpose.**

If the Higher Power wanted to have someone to love, we must be worth loving. Believe in love; believe in yourself. The gift waiting at the end of the path is the original *you*! Don't be afraid. You are a masterpiece worth discovering. In this chapter, I am going to suggest you get out a journal and complete a few exercises to further your transformation process toward realizing dreams.

CHILDREN AT PLAY EXERCISE

Let's look way back to the beginning when we were children. One of the best ways to discover your true self is to look back when you were little by how you played. One time, I knew a kid who loved to draw. He was three years old and he would draw all day long. I noticed his parents would detour him from drawing and try to put him in sports. He was very shy and did not seem to like sports, but eventually grew accustomed to it. Those parents did not seek to do anything wrong, however, sometimes we are detoured from who we truly are when people try to make us something we are not. ***One of the greatest things we can do as parents is study who our children already are and reflect to them who we see*** versus trying to make them someone they are not. Take out your journal and answer the following questions:

- ➢ How did you play?
- ➢ What did you like or not like?
- ➢ What was your personality like back then?
- ➢ How are you different now versus back then?

When I look back at playing, I played *teacher* with my dolls. I played *orphanage director* with my dolls. I ran a *real-estate business,* answering the phone as if I were the broker. I loved playing where it required imagination, playing outside under trees and building forts. I was a very sensitive, empathic child. When I played, the theme was that I was in charge of groups where I would teach, nurture, and care for people. What I did not like as a child was anything where I was required to perform individually or being put on the spot. We all come from imperfect parents. To become *self-actualized*, we need to learn to *re-parent* ourselves. Now that you are in tune with how you played, let us look at how you felt.

RE-PARENTING YOURSELF EXERCISE

One of the greatest ways to come to *self-actualization,* recondition ourselves to become who we really are, and meet the needs that were unfulfilled in childhood is to ***re-parent*** ourselves. We will come further faster on our journey by doing this.

To re-parent ourselves we must constantly be in touch with how we feel. Our feelings are telling us something and we need to take responsibility for how we feel and give ourselves what we *need*. This is the greatest way to get to know ourselves; to figure out who we are.

Take out your journal and a picture of yourself when you were around six years old. If you do not have a picture, imagine a scene or a picture you saw of yourself around that age. Complete a fifteen-minute exercise. Look at the picture and ask yourself the following questions:

> ➢ What do I observe about the little boy/little girl in the picture?

> ➢ What else do I observe in the picture?

> ➢ What does the little boy/little girl need at that age? (Reflect back on what you needed.)

> ➢ How can I, the adult, give him/her what they need?

Many of us stay handicapped in life because of needs we did not get met as children. This exercise is so that you can identify those needs and then act as the new parent to your inner child. When we take responsibility for parenting the child inside of us, several things start to happen. We soon realize we can give our inner child exactly what he/she needs. When we do this, our child-self and our adult-self begin to integrate. Here is a practical example of how to do this.

Imagine a woman is married and her husband abuses her emotionally. The woman desires to be close to her husband, but he constantly pushes her away. When he was a child and things went well, his parents would play with him and then turn on him and degrade him. In marriage, when things go well with his wife, he fulfills his script and turns on her by belittling her before she can turn against him. He didn't realize that protecting himself hurt his wife.

When this wife *re-parents* herself, she would identify her hurt, put her little girl self in a chair, and talk to her as if she were her mom. She would say something like this, *I understand he was mean to you. I understand you desire to be close to him. I understand you feel hurt. I am with you. You are not alone.* Any time we feel hurt by another person, we need to take the time and act as a parent to ourselves and give ourselves exactly what we need, perhaps what we wished our mom or dad would have done. We need to talk daily to the inner child until it becomes second nature.

Each one of us was from some type of dysfunctional family, having needs that were never met. If our main needs of being loved and wanted were not met, we are left now seeking those needs to be met in unhealthy ways. Many of us have been abused in obvious ways: physically, sexually, intellectually, and emotionally. Some of us have been abused in passive, less obvious ways by being ignored or neglected. Most of us have experienced some type of trauma. Whether it is death, divorce, or any other loss, it comes to all of us. Some of us experienced trauma when we were young, sometimes too young to remember. Our whole personality can be based on coping with trauma, potentially causing personality disorders.

For any of us seeking authenticity to see our dreams realized, it is key to continue to get in touch with the inner child and see how the child feels. We must continue to nurture and parent the inner child to meet his or her basic needs. Identifying and taking care of our inner child is essential to knowing who we are.

The more people are able to get in touch with their inner children, identify how they feel, and meet their own needs instead of getting it from outside sources, the more they and their circumstances will change. People will tolerate abuse less. People will stop using drugs. People will stick up for themselves. People will quit jobs they do not like.

When we begin to take care of our own needs instead of depending on others, we become who we are and do what we were meant to do. Put your inner child in a chair beside you, now you the adult, must talk to the child. Every single day we need to take responsibility for the child inside of us by nurturing, comforting, and giving the child exactly what the child needs.

DEAR DAD/DEAR MOM LETTER

When we begin to get in touch with the unmet needs of the inner child, we are often faced with anger or resentment toward the person who hurt the inner child. This is where you can take out your journal and write a letter to the person who was your primary source of pain. When you write this letter, say whatever you want, however you want.

Note: *DO NOT GIVE THE LETTER TO THE PERSON; IT IS ONLY FOR YOU.* It is for the inner child. Get your journal out and write a letter regarding the following:

> ➢ What did your inner child experience that brought you pain?

> ➢ How did your inner child feel?

> ➢ What did your inner child dislike about the person who brought you pain?

> ➢ What did your inner child like about the person who brought you pain? (if anything)

> What did the pain this person caused do to your inner child?

> How can you the adult, give your inner child *now* what the child needed *then*?

An example: We discover that the child felt unloved and insecure most of his/her life. The adult, *YOU,* need to constantly talk to the *child* in you and tell the child, *"I am with you."* Offer words of comfort, *"No one can hurt you now. I am taking care of you."* Offer words of encouragement such as, *"You are important and good enough."* Protect the child inside of you by saying, *"Don't put yourself in that situation, it will hurt you."* We need to think of ourselves daily in the same manner as if we were caring for a little child.

DEAR GOD LETTER

Lastly, take out a journal and write a letter to God asking Him to help you forgive those who have hurt you. Feel the pain. Validate the pain and comfort your inner child. Leave those who have hurt you to God. Those who have hurt you no longer have power over you. Remind the inner child they cannot hurt you anymore. We are the new parent of the inner child. It is our responsibility now to *care for ourselves*.

This was the process I followed to discover the real me. Many people have gone through this process and discovered the real them. You can go through this process and discover *the real you*. This process will set you free from others so that you can be in touch with the authentic you. Discovering yourself is essential. This is where you will begin to dream, believe, and see Divine Destiny!

Chapter 11-Dream on and never give up!

Now that you have thought back to being little, what were some of your dreams back then? What dreams do you have now? Don't ever give up on dreaming. You were dreamed into existence and you are meant to dream. My husband, Dr. Richard Amato has shouted to the nations, *"If you can dream it, you can achieve it. If you can imagine it, you can become it."* Moreover, his granddaughter, Grace Olivia Zabik cheers, *"There is so much more!"*

Take out your journal and write a list of your dreams. Imagine if nothing was in your way what you would dream about. As you dream, there will be storms.

With storms come sorrow. And sorrow *will* eventually turn into sunshine.

DREAMING WHEN YOU HAVE BEEN ABUSED

For those of you who have looked at your inner child, you may have discovered that you were abused. Being abused can no doubt, inhibit us from dreaming. In those cases, we need to take the time to heal by getting the licensed professional help that we need. Expect life to give you a double portion of blessing for your trouble. Don't let the past hurt and shame keep you from dreaming. Those who have abused us gave us a clear message through their abuse that we did not deserve good; they were wrong. Surrender to the fact that good is coming to you. We are no longer victims of other people; we are victors when we take responsibility of our inner child. Let go of everyone except yourself; *let go and let God.* Choose to believe you are worth your dreams coming true.

My sister Desi was brought into our family because my grandfather Ervin called my dad one day and told him that Desi was living in an extremely traumatic situation. Desi was by blood my cousin; however, she became my real sister.

My parents received Desi and John, her blood brother, as their own children when they were seven and nine years of age. They were poor, mistreated, and abused. Coming to live with their new parents changed their lives forever. Their world went from rags to riches, and from hopeless to hopeful. Desi wants you to know, ***"What you want exists. Don't settle until you get it!"***

LIES THAT BLOCK OUR DREAMS
- ❖ They will change and love me one day.
- ❖ If I do better, they will do better.
- ❖ I am worthless.
- ❖ I cannot do anything on my own.
- ❖ I am a victim who is helpless.
- ❖ I am trapped.
- ❖ I am not in control.
- ❖ I can't move forward.
- ❖ If I forgive them, I am saying it was okay for them to abuse me.

BEING TRAPPED IS AN ILLUSION

When we feel trapped, we desire to go forward, but we believe we are stuck. Although we are unhappy, we feel incapable of doing something about it. When this happens, we are miserable on the inside and can live miserably for many years. We do not see a way out when we feel trapped. *No one is truly trapped unless someone is holding them against their will.* Feeling trapped is when you want to quit something and no longer be a part of it but are afraid of the repercussions.

We fear we may put ourselves in a situation worse than the one we are currently in. Do you want to stop feeling trapped? *Fear keeps people in trapped situations and fear is the enemy to dreams coming true.* Low self-esteem tells people they do not deserve a better life.

Often people stay in trapped situations because they don't want to do the work required to get out of it or because they really *want* to stay in the situation. *Those who want to stay in trapped situations get a "reward" they are not aware of.* An example of this would be staying with an alcoholic spouse because they distract you from yourself and staying with an abusive man because he pays all of your bills. We are delusional when we stay in trapped situations expecting others to change. The only real healthy option is to move forward and do the next right thing for you. If the people you want to change are with you, they will join you by getting healthy and if they don't join you, they will most likely get rid of you. Some people would rather stay sick. The process of this will show you the truth. Take one little step at a time and move forward to fulfilling your dreams. Choose gratitude instead of fear. After taking one small step at a time, you will get to where you are trying to go.

NEVER GIVE UP!

Thomas Edison invented a light bulb. He may have failed more than one thousand times before he got the light bulb to work but eventually his invention contributed light to all of our lives. Thomas Edison never gave up. *Walt Disney* may have gone bankrupt several times but eventually he created Disney Land. Walt Disney never gave up. *Ben Carson* may have had a rough start when he was born to a young mother. He may have had a rough start because of bad grades and a bad temper. Perhaps because of his mom's tough love and discipline, his grades began to rise. Eventually, one step at a time, he became a world-renowned pediatric surgeon. He never gave up.

When my niece was ten years old, Ben Carson, who depends greatly on God, saved her life by removing a tumor from her brain. My brother John, Emily's father, would tell you he could not have made it through that situation without the strength of his God. My entire family is glad *Ben Carson never gave up!* Penny Amato Richardson always says, ***"Do all you possibly can, the best you possibly can, as long as you possibly can. Do your best, and with God leave the rest."***

James Cash Penney was a poor minister's son from Missouri. He wanted to be a lawyer but found himself in sales. Because of failed health, he went to a dryer climate in Missouri and found employment. His employment allowed him to make money and open a business. He had a few businesses fail and he also had two wives die. While he was known as a man of integrity, he suffered many hardships. He always wanted to open up a successful business. He did and then landed his biggest business of all called JCPenney. James Penney never gave up! Dreaming requires indefatigable determination! You must be relentless in the pursuit of your dreams. *Oprah Winfrey says, "The biggest adventure you can take is to live the life of your dreams."* [13]

THE SUCCESS OF ANCIENT DREAMERS

Noah had a dream of saving his family. He had to build an ark. He and his family were saved. Because their family was saved, the human race continued. *Abraham* had a dream of fathering a nation. Abraham had to be willing to sacrifice his son. He had to make the decision to leave everything he had, all his comfort, and follow God; he was tested. He became the father of many nations. *David* defeated Goliath. He was a shepherd boy, who had to fight the lion, while protecting his sheep. This prepared him to fight Goliath. He was faithful in the little and God gave him much. David believed God and won.

Joshua felt unqualified to take over for Moses, but God promised to be with him. Joshua obeyed exactly what he was told. There were instructions Joshua *did not understand* but he did it anyway. He chose to obey. They had to march around a wall for seven days. On the seventh day, the wall fell, and they won the battle. Joshua passed the test, never gave up, and won!

Jesus Christ of Nazareth sweated blood, was beaten, suffered and crucified to fulfill His destiny, which was to die on the cross. He claimed to be the *King of the Jews* who came to die to *save* us and *forgive* us of our sins. He went through astronomical suffering all the way to death, becoming the final victim and the greatest victor who ever lived to take away the sins of the world. Jesus Christ never gave up!

Whether you see these stories as literal or symbolic, these inspirational and illuminating stories in history can give you strength, courage, and hope to inspire you to not

give up. Don't be an *idiot* by giving up on your dreams.

Never ever give up as you are marked with Divine Des-

tiny. The person you are deep down inside is begging to

come out and be free. Don't give up on your dreams be-

cause your dreams are meant to be.

Chapter 12-Dreams really do come true!

Rarely have we seen anyone fail who *"trusts God, cleans house, and helps others."* Many of those who have had mental disturbances and extreme emotional pain do recover when they are capable of being honest with themselves. Getting honest means, we are no longer an idiot, handicapped by the way we were conditioned, we are free! We used to be disabled and now we are able! *We are now doing something we have never done before and now we have something we have never had before.* I found through my counseling experience, that once people lived by faith, not religion, identified and changed their negative childhood scripts, and proceeded to help other people, their dreams literally did come true! Years later, I discovered that

Alcoholics Anonymous had a saying for those who wanted to stay sober, *"Trust God, clean house, and help others."*[14] It dawned on me we were saying the same thing. The very steps that can help a drug addict and alcoholic stay sober are the same steps to help any person realize their dreams.

WHILE YOU WAIT, TRUST GOD

Trusting God was essential to becoming a single mother. Staying where I was would have cost me my very own life, therefore, I had no other choice than to leave. The journey the children and I went on was *priceless*. We learned together, that in our home, ***God was my Husband and He was our Father.*** He proved Himself to us and took very good care of us. He provided every step of the way, without fail or exception. Next, I had to trust God just to look at myself. Eventually, I realized I was scared to death of me. I truly didn't know who I was. I had been living in the shadows of other people my entire life telling me what to do and who to be. I had to step out in faith and put my life into the care of God. Finally, I was able to get into a recovery program for codependency and seek my inner child.

WHILE YOU WAIT, CLEAN HOUSE

When I first faced myself, I told a friend, *"I have no idea how I will get this running negative script out of my head."* Although I was unaware of it for some time, *belittling myself* like others had become a regular pattern of mine. Finally, I began to *re-parent* the little girl inside of me and *nurture* my inner child. For the first time in my life, instead of concentrating on others, pleasing them, or worrying about what they thought, I was cleaning my own house. The *old me* was being cleaned out so the *authentic me* could appear. This process came through individual counseling, codependent groups, and the process of the exercises in this book. What worked for me is the reason I share with you.

WHILE YOU WAIT, GO HELP OTHERS

It is amazing what can happen when we step out in faith, turn our lives over to the care of God, and go help others. There was a man who went through the transformation process of counseling. So much of him changed and many of his dreams came true-except one. He worried himself sick, regarding finances, knowing that his job would soon come to an end. His dream was to get a new job, but he felt it was impossible because of a past criminal record. He did the work of cleaning out his core, put his trust in God, and daily put out resumes but seemed unable to find new employment. There was nothing either one of us could think of that he could do.

I shared about the faithfulness of God, assured him it did not matter what he had done, and reminded him God was reliable and would take care of him. Like my brother Greg Drennan says, *"Regardless of what they have done, family always takes care of family."* God, our *daddy,* takes care of us. We ended the therapeutic rela-

tionship with me saying, *"Keep trusting God, keep mak-*

ing personal progress, put out the resumes, and go help

someone!" Right before he left counseling, he told me he

began helping an ill man in his neighborhood. The disease

made it impossible for him to get around. I thought to my-

self, *"Good, at least helping another person will help him*

get out of thinking about himself." His old job *did not*

end when he left counseling. That is where we left off.

   Years later, I received a call from that man who ex-

plained that after he left counseling, two things happened:

The ill man he had been helping sadly passed away, and

he finally lost his job. At that point, he still did not have

new employment. Much to his surprise, the ill man had no

family and left him his entire inheritance! Not a day went

by that my client's bills were not paid. Soon after that, he

got new employment which was better than the job he had

before. Things naturally work out when we trust God,

clean our insides, and help others. Alcoholics Anonymous states, *"No matter how far down the scale we have gone, we will see how our experience can benefit others."* [6] We never know how God will showcase his faithfulness; we just know He will.

DREAMS MODELED

Dreaming big dreams has been passed down to me from my family heritage. On my mother's side, my grandfather Ervin T. Rouse was a poor North Carolina boy. He passed away when I was six. He was known as a *trick fiddler*. He fascinated me and others when he played the violin. I have yet to see a person put the bow in between his legs, with the violin held upside down, and play a piece of music like he did. He took his love of the violin and having fun to a whole new level. While living in a shack in Florida, he wrote the song called the *Orange Blossom Special.* Many considered his song the *#1 blue grass song of the century* in the year 2000. Although he maintained his humble living, he made so much money just by having fun. To this day, his children continue to receive a very nice inheritance! Ervin's example taught me that *knowing who we are and doing what we love are important to fulfilling our dreams.*

On my father's side, Georgia, his oldest sibling, is the matriarch of the Drennan clan. The Drennan family was a poor family from Ohio. When Aunt Georgia was seventeen years old, she left everything she knew, trusted God, and moved to Maryland. Through her ambitious spirit and a lot of prayer, she was able to get jobs for our entire family. Aunt Georgia, very determined, led the way and both my father, (her little brother) and my mother followed her. My dad died a wealthy man. Aunt Georgia changed the monetary needs of an entire generation. And more importantly *Aunt Georgia left us with a heritage of faith!*

Aunt Georgia is a *big-time-operator* and what stands behind her operation is faith in God. She taught us that God is the giver of all things. Georgia became the *Director of Facilities and Management* at the top union in Washington D. C. called, *The American Federation of Labor and Congress of Industrial Organizations (AFL-CIO)*. God gave to Aunt Georgia and she gave back to God. *I will remember her as one of the most giving people I have ever known.*

Through her lifestyle, she taught us that God cares deeply for every person. She believes every person is lovable and continues to teach that God will take care of each and every one of our needs. My Aunt Georgia wants the world to know, *"God is true to His promises. We can trust Him absolutely!"*

INFLUENCING MANY GENERATIONS

All of us are afforded the opportunity to influence the generations, like my grandfather Ervin who inspired us to make money by having fun while using our natural giftedness, and my Aunt Georgia who influenced us to leave home, follow God, and have faith. Their messages passed on through generations to the children and grandchildren. This was recently proven when I asked my twelve-year-old son Andrew the question, *"If you were to give one message to inspire the world, what it would be?"* He said, **"Don't worry. Be happy!"** So, then I asked him, *"Why would you want to tell others not to worry and to be happy?"* He answered, matter of fact, **"Because God provides!"** This was profound in my mind. My eighty-two-year-old aunt taught us that God provides and now my twelve-year-old son with no prompting or conversation beforehand answered the question-*because God provides.*

Therefore, I tell you that ***you may not like where you came from, but you for sure can change where you will go.*** Not only could you direct yourself to somewhere different, but you could influence many generations to go somewhere different as well. When we clean up ourselves, trust God, and help others, we will see that we can make a difference for years to come.

MY CHILDHOOD INFLUENCES

My sister, Jennifer Drennan, had a very large influence on my life growing up. Aunt Georgia, who noticed her love of jewelry when she would wear ten necklaces as a child, influenced her to invest in what she loved, and helped her start her own jewelry business. At eighteen years of age, Jennifer became a jeweler, selling the best fine jewelry, offering the best deals out there. She is a natural born salesperson who also became the best realtor in MD, VA, and D.C, who works with Taylor Properties.

God used my sister's persuasive personality to teach me several things. First, the faith she learned from Aunt Georgia was passed down to me as she constantly assured me that God would take care of me and meet my needs. The second was that she greatly influenced me with my self-esteem. Jennifer always said, ***"You are perfect just the way God made you and being who you are makes you the best."*** Sissy was *my little mamma.* She clearly influenced me to be a very goal-oriented person and taught me by example to dream, believe, and achieve.

My father majorly influenced my spirituality and love for counseling. His lifestyle displayed that *people are important.* My mother modeled being a lady, as well as, a supportive wife. For years, I watched my mom support my dad, thus, once again, showcasing the message, *people are important.* My mom taught us to care about what God thought as she modeled an entire lifetime of serving others. The greatest thing I will remember about my mother is that no matter what, I could always count on her to be *the mother hen.* Both of my parents were dreamers, believers, and achievers who supported their children and grandchildren, including monetarily help, to fulfill their dreams. Gratitude is my attitude for a heritage of faith.

My dad's greatest joy was his babies. My mom's greatest gifts were her children. Both of my parents made *kids* the priority. Just like my dad, my babies are my joy. And just like my mom, we will die **the mother hens**.

MY CHILDHOOD DREAMS

All I can remember about being a child is that I loved babies and wanted to have them one day. In the eighth grade, I began dreaming. First, I dreamed of getting married to a man who would *love* me and be my *best friend;* where the two of us could *help people together*. Second, I dreamed of having children of my own and planned to run a daycare business in my home, so I could stay home with them. Thirdly, I dreamed of getting a license in counseling and opening up a private practice. Years after dreaming about my life came marriage, at a very young age, and then came the privilege of birthing three children.

The next decade was spent running a daycare business in my home where I was afforded the opportunity of staying home with my children. Some of the greatest times of my life were spent with those precious children. Watching my babies grow brought me much joy. And finally, I was able to get a counseling license. Little did I know, I would become licensed in Maryland, Virginia, Michigan, and Florida and establish a non-profit. Counseling has been the most rewarding career of my life. And then, unknown to me, there was even a bigger dream.

GOD'S DREAM

Private practice always seemed like the best way to do counseling. During the transition, before we got to Florida, it became clear that God wanted me to do things differently, by establishing a 501(c)(3), tax-deductible, non-profit. The benefit of this would be that people could donate and we could give to those in need. The process was very rigid and lasted eighteen months until approval was given. Being in the midst of my own personal trauma, the idea was far from appealing. Several times, before moving to Florida, I dreamed of counseling buildings and conference centers that said the words *Dream Believe Counseling* and *Dream Believe Conference Center* on the buildings and billboards.

In my dreams, there was a girl walking with me and she would say, *"Look up,"* and I would stand aghast at what I saw. When I awoke from these dreams, I literally cried and said, *"God, I don't want that. You know what I want."* This was God's dream, not mine. Although one of my personal dreams had not yet unfolded, God's unexpected dream of the *Dream Believe* non-profit was established in April of 2012. We proceeded on with trusting God, cleaning house, and we are helping people now more than ever. The joy that manifests itself, from God's dream, continues to live on daily in our counseling practice as we watch people's dreams come true.

THE GREATEST DREAM OF ALL

Once the business got started, I was in counseling and meeting with recovery groups, more than ever. And through the transformation process, something happened; *I came to love myself.* There are no words to describe the difference in how I feel. Life taught me that the greatest dream of all is loving yourself. *Loving yourself is the KEY to seeing your dreams come true.*

In all the dreams I had, loving myself was never my dream. In times past, I thought happiness came from other people or good things happening. Instead, what I found was that happiness came from accepting myself and being me. When I stopped long enough to look for me, I found me. To face myself was the scariest adventure on Earth, yet at the end of the rainbow, there was *gold...ME!* Now, there is transformation process waiting for you. There is a priceless gift to be found... *YOU!* After much counseling, groups, and personal recovery, I ended up facilitating twenty-seven groups a week in rehabs and invested much of my time helping alcoholics, codependents and their families. The work of helping others through the drug epidemic brought me further and faster to my long, lost dream.

THE INVENTOR'S TIMETABLE OF 7 YEARS

The amount of time for a dream to come true is not always on our timetable. My oldest son Michael says, **"When times get tough, that's when our best selves' come to fruition."** Sometimes it is the tough times that create and make our dreams. After spending seven years of my life being a single mother, the day came when a long, lost dream of mine, perhaps one that I had given up on, came true. I married a man who *loves* me and who is my *best friend*. **Being married doesn't fulfill the dream of marriage. Two individuals who love themselves and each other make the marriage a dream.**

Dr. Richard Amato, the founder of the War on Addiction, has lived an entire life of faith and is the greatest husband ever. He is the husband God picked for me and he is perfect. We have laughed and had more fun together than in an entire lifetime.

Richard Stanley Amato is *precious!* It is my privilege to know him and be with him. He has taught me more than any other human and has an absolutely incredible mind. Many consider him the *Einstein of the Bible*. His biological children brag about the amazing dad he has been, and his grandchildren can't get enough of him. He is the best stepfather ever! He has modeled after our faithful God who provides for his children. He has not only provided for his children and my children; he has provided for the poor and afflicted children around the world. And it is now our honor to help people. *Together* we founded ***Dream, Believe Institute!***

.

THE DREAM LIVES ON

Dr. Richard Amato and I are Clergy and Licensed Mental Health Counselors in Wellington, Florida. We both have a passion to help addicts and those who love them recover from the horrendous brain disease of addiction. With over forty-six years' experience between us, our international travels together have helped us see that humans afflicted with addiction and those who love them are treatable and curable. In fact, those afflicted with addiction become the most productive members of any country and any culture by getting help from a recovery program that works. Both Dr. Richard and I went through our own individual transformation process. The transformation process was worth it. And dreams really do come true!

"It is now our Divine Destiny together-to help you see that you have one!"

Don't ever give up on dreaming as you are meant to dream. *Begin dreaming about loving yourself.* As you go through the transformation process of loving yourself, you will naturally see your dreams realized. We are here to believe for you until you can believe for yourself. We are here to walk with you through this process. You may call Dream Believe Institute at **1-855-SET-FREE** to get the help that you need. Do not be an idiot living with unnecessary handicaps. Believe what Ivan Pavlov discovered that you have been conditioned. Get help to recondition yourself and see that Divine Destiny is waiting for you!

REFERENCES

1. Handicapped (2019). *Dictionary.com.* Accessed October 27, 2018 through http://www.dictionary.com/browse/handicapped

2. Interpolation (2019). *Interpolation.* Accessed October 27, 2018 through https://en.wikipedia.org/wiki/Interpolation

3. McGraw, Phil (Dr. Phil). *"My dad used to say, 'You wouldn't worry so much about what people thought of you, if you knew how seldom they did'."* August 17, 2013, 11:13 AM. Tweet.

4. Bustanoby A. (1978). *But I Didn't Want a Divorce: Putting Your Life Back Together.* Grand rapids: Zondervan

5. Readout of First Lady Melania Trump's Participation in an Opioid Town Hall at Liberty University. (2018). Accessed November 28, 2018 through https://www.whitehouse.gov/briefings-statements/readout-first-lady-melania-trumps-participation-opioid-town-hall-liberty-university

6. Wilson, B. (1939). *Alcoholics Anonymous: The story of how many thousands of men and women have recovered from alcoholism* (1st ed.). New York City: Alcoholics Anonymous World Services.

7. Kind (2019). *Merriam-webster.com.* Accessed February 9, 2019 through https://www.merriam-webster.com/dictionary/kind

8. Aerosmith (1973). *Dream On* [CD]. Intermedia Studios: Adrian Barber. (1972)

9. Transformation (2019). *Dictionary.com.* Accessed February 9, 2019 through https://www.diction-ary.com/browse/transform
10. Lee, J (1981). Lookin for love. On *Lookin for love* [CD]. S.i.: Asylum Records. (1980)
11. Marcus, W. M. (2018). *The priestly prayer of the blessing.* Lake Mary, FL: Charisma House
12. Clinton, T. E., & Sprinkle, P. (2012). *Break through: When to give in, how to push back.* Brentwood, TN: Worthy Publishing.
13. What Oprah Knows for Sure About Life's Biggest Adventure (2002). Accessed February 9, 2019 through http://www.oprah.com/spirit/what-oprah-knows-for-sure-about-lifes-biggest-adventure
14. Alcoholics Anonymous World Services, Inc. (2001). *ALCOHOLICS ANONYMOUS* (4th ed.). New York, NY: ALCOHOLICS ANONYMOUS SERVICES.

Biography

My father, Robert E. Drennan, Jr., was a marriage and family counselor under whom I was privileged to study counseling. Every minute of his counseling groups that I attended (beginning thirteen years of age) was thoroughly enjoyed.

My master's program in counseling began in 2004 and my father passed away in 2005. Throughout my whole life, I considered him the **greatest counselor on the earth,** which was definitely confirmed to me when I attended his funeral.

The funeral went hours past the scheduled time, with over 500 people there who gave beautiful testimonies. *"I had over thirty years of depression until I counseled with Bob."* Others said, *"Bob helped me with panic attacks,"* and *"Bob saved our marriage."* The testimonies continued so long the funeral had to be kicked out of the church as there were other scheduled events that day. As I heard what the people shared, I stood amazed that he was my biological father. This book was written with the privilege of knowing *I come with the wisdom of a grey-haired man.* Much credit is given to my father for what he taught me; he will go down in history as my counseling hero.

I received my master's degree in counseling in 2006. I am also licensed in the states of Maryland, Virginia, Michigan and Florida and have supervised an upwards of twenty-one counselors at a time. My expertise is in communication skills, marriage counseling and extensive work with addiction and codependency. My clientele has been the intelligence community, patients with trauma at hospitals, private practice, community counseling, and addicts in rehabilitation centers.

Rev. Dr. Richard Amato, my precious husband and spiritual hero is an internationally renowned speaker and founder and president of *RAMCare*, a multi-million-dollar, non-profit humanitarian and educational organization. Dr. Amato and his teams have traveled extensively in Russia, China, Cuba, and other post-socialist countries where he personally met with Presidents Gorbachev and Yeltsin in the Kremlin. Dr. Amato has traveled in over sixty countries and in almost all fifty states as well as the Virgin Islands. He has spoken face-to-face to well over a million junior and senior high public-school students, giving the message *"The Power of a Choice"* regarding bullying and addiction.

Dr. Amato is an expert on the brain disease of addiction with a master's degree in Human Services Counseling: Addictions and Recovery. Much credit is given to my precious husband, for all he has taught me, regarding how to work with addicts and those who love them.

Dr. Richard and I are Clinical Clergy and Licensed Mental Health Counselors in Wellington, Florida with a passion to help addicts and those who love them recover from the horrendous brain disease of addiction. With over 46 years of experience between us, we offer a recovery program that works. We also work with families and help couples get off the *'carousel ride'* of the mundane life called marriage. We train counselors in both marriage and family as well as addiction and codependency. Together, we founded **Dream Believe Institute,** where we practice a holistic approach to counseling to help people realize their dreams.

Dream Believe Institute (DBI) is a holistic healing center where we offer mental health counseling for individuals, couples and families as well as training for counselors working on licensure. We believe in order to have a total life transformation, people must deal with both symptom management as well as the trauma that has created root issues.

DBI helps addicts manage the brain disease of addiction, to get the freedom they deserve, and helps codependents find the serenity they deserve. We teach couples how to have a happy marriage. *DBI* offers tools for each individual, on how to live one day at a time, so they may experience peace, joy and contentment, fulfilling a life of realized dreams.

The Power behind my father, my husband and I, is a Power greater than ourselves. We could have done nothing without God. He, ultimately, is our greatest Hero and the reason for which we can do all things. He is the Dream-Maker and the Dream-Fulfiller of our lives.

1-855-SET-FREE

dreambelieveinstitute.com

WE NEED *YOUR* HELP
TO SAVE THE YOUTH OF AMERICA!

**People with addiction issues
are not just those living under a bridge.
Addiction has robbed our Presidents,
our Teachers, our Counselors, our Doctors,
our Moms, our Dads,
and now OUR CHILDREN!**

Dr. Richard Amato, the founder of the War on Addiction, has spoken to millions of young people and adults around the world. Thousands have been delivered from the disease of addiction and countless numbers of young people report that they escaped the temptation of their first use of alcohol or drugs. Now, he has targeted the middle and high school students in all fifty states and focused on Palm Beach County, Florida schools. He will be speaking about the biggest bully of all, ever recorded in history-
ADDICTION.

YOUR DONATION IS TAX-DEDUCTIBLE

**Dream Believe Institute (DBI)
1035 S. State Road 7
Wellington, FL 33414
or
donate online:
https://www.dreambelieveinstitute.com/donations**

Made in the USA
Las Vegas, NV
02 July 2024

91769926R00132